Portraits of "the Whiteman"

Linguistic play and cultural symbols
among the Western Apache

Portraits of "the Whiteman"

Linguistic play and cultural symbols
among the Western Apache

Keith H. Basso

Department of Anthropology
University of Arizona

Illustrations by Vincent Craig

Cambridge University Press

Cambridge
London   New York   Melbourne

Published by the Syndics of the Cambridge University Press
The Pitt Building, Trumpington Street, Cambridge CB2 1RP
Bentley House, 200 Euston Road, London NW1 2DB
32 East 57th Street, New York, NY 10022, USA
296 Beaconsfield Parade, Middle Park, Melbourne 3206, Australia

© Cambridge University Press 1979

First Published 1979

Printed in the United States of America
Typeset by Jay's Publishers Services, Inc., No. Scituate, Mass.
Printed and bound by
Lithocrafters Inc., Chelsea, Mich.

Library of Congress Cataloging in Publication Data
Basso, Keith H   1940–
Portraits of "the Whiteman"
Bibliography: p.
1. Apache Indians – Joking.
2. Apache wit and humor – History and criticism.
3. Indians of North America – Arizona – Joking.
4. Americans – Anecdotes, facetiae, satire, etc. I. Title.
E99.A6B2295 970'.004'97 78–31535
ISBN 0 521 22640 6 hard covers
ISBN 0 521 29593 9 paperback

*For three Apaches, now gone away, who
encouraged me to laugh at myself:*

Leon Beatty
Percy Peaches
Teddy Peaches

And for ten others who showed me how:

Ned Anderson
Delmar Boni
Morely Cromwell
Francis Dehose
Ernest Murphy
Dudley Patterson
Alvin Quay
Roy Quay
Calvert Tessay
Nashley Tessay

Contents

Foreword

When Keith Basso sent me his manuscript, it came as a gift, a gift of laughter. The fourth portrait especially dissolved me in delight, and delighted others with whom I shared it. When he invited me to write this Foreword, I found myself "gifted" again.[1] There came a feather that a Cibecue friend had blessed. That unexpected symbol of reciprocity was dissolving too, making one for a moment light as breath. So it is twice a privilege, and responsibility, to share in presenting these portraits of 'the Whiteman'.

The portraits speak for themselves, and Vincent Craig's cartoons make meanings immediate as well. The significance of the portraits to the understanding of Indian Americans and to the general understanding of culture is lucidly stated in the text. Like any seasoned scholar, of course, I can mention references that the author did not choose to include, and will. What I can best do, I think, is to try to highlight in words of my own the fact that the portraits do speak for themselves, while enlarging upon the context and importance of the fact.

The Apache portraits of 'the Whiteman' have analogues elsewhere in Indian country (cf. n. 21 of this book), but that is not often recognized. The great capacity of Indian people for creative wit has been obscured by the image of the Indian as silent stoic. Elsewhere Basso has helped us recognize that silence is a function of definition of situation (1970), as has his colleague, Susan Philips (1972,

1975). The general point was noted long ago by Washington Irving, writing in the context of a tour on the prairies in 1832 among the Osage, but has had to be rediscovered and given substance today.

Here is Irving's report (1865: 51–2):

> [They] occasionally indulge in a vein of comic humor and dry satire, to which the Indians appear to me much more prone than is generally imagined.
>
> In fact, the Indians that I have had an opportunity of seeing in real life are quite different from those described in poetry. They are by no means the stoics that they are represented; taciturn, unbending, without a tear or a smile. Taciturn they are, it is true, when in company with white men, whose good-will they distrust, and whose language they do not understand; but the white man is equally taciturn under like circumstances. When the Indians are among themselves, however, there cannot be greater gossips. Half their time is taken up in talking over their adventures in war and hunting, and in telling whimsical stories. They are great mimics and buffoons, also, and entertain themselves excessively at the expense of the whites with whom they have associated, and who have supposed them impressed with profound respect for their grandeur and dignity. They are curious observers, noting everything in silence, but with a keen and watchful eye; occasionally exchanging a glance or a grunt with each other, when anything particularly strikes them; but reserving all comments until they are alone. Then it is that they give full scope to criticism, satire, mimicry, and mirth.

More than a century later, it can still be a secret or a surprise, even to those who live alongside Indians and teach their children, that there is this flow of wit among them.

There are many in the United States who still need to be ignorant of the real Indian people living near them, even while admiring Indians remote in place or time. One can understand the need to think this way on the part of people who could not ponder comfortably the fact that their land or livelihood is bound up with what Indians living near them have lost. But scholars bear a responsibility too. Too often we have written about Indians as a collective type, "the Navajo," "the Hopi," etc., rather than as individual personalities. One writes about the "the Clackamas" and "Clackamas mythology," for example, rather than about the myths in Clackamas of Mrs. Victoria Howard, the only person whose myths in Clackamas are known to us. It takes a fine-grained attention, the kind that portraits of 'whiteman' demand, to catch the individual voice. And the devices that Indian people use to catch individual traits, to mark personality types, have not much been noted. The early attention to these things of Edward Sapir remains rather exceptional, and Sapir recorded only the devices of marking, not the enactments, as does this path-breaking book.[2]

It also is a question of more than a single field trip. Keith Basso's relationship with Western Apache people has been sustained for many years. To be sure, it was the luck of a tape recorder's being left on that revealed a performance, and the book makes clear that performance is likely only among certain people under certain circumstances, sustained for only a moment. One can come from the kitchen, as it were, and find, as in William Carlos Williams's poem "The artist" (1954: 43), "But the show was over." Even with the luck of the tape, to have the person involved insist on providing a full account of the event is not luck; it is confidence, trust.

I can attest that the portraits do communicate. When Keith's manuscript came, I had reached a point in teaching

"The ethnography of speaking" to which a portrait of 'the Whiteman' was marvelously apt. With such pronunciation of Apache as phonetic training permitted, and a sense of English style transferred from Warm Springs, one had only to do the lines. Students got the point directly; a foundation in sociolinguistics was absorbed through laughter.

It is fundamental to sociolinguistics to identify and understand differences in what Goffman has called "the nature of deference and demeanor" (1962). It ought to be fundamental to all understanding of language to attend to enactment, including intonation, tone of voice, accompanying gesture, all the communicative modalities that began to be analyzed as "paralinguistics" and "kinesics" a generation ago. The need to bring these two concerns together leads two pioneers of the field, John Gumperz and Jenny Cook-Gumperz, to single out the link under the term *contextualization of discourse*. The two concerns are together already in Apache portraits of 'the Whiteman'. Nor is this simply because all instances of verbal interaction necessarily involve such meanings and such means. The two concerns are together, not only as behavior, but also as analysis. The portraits are an expressive genre that embodies an analysis.

The relevance to social theory of the kind of enacted analysis present in these portraits cannot be overstated. Even today we tend to miss the presence of analytic understanding in non-Western cultures whenever it does not take the form of a vocabulary. Even so stimulating and shrewd a theorist as Pierre Bourdieu (1977) appears to think of the Algerian peasants among whom he lived, and by extension, of the practical life of most peoples known to anthropology, as in principle in a state of *doxa,* of unquestioning acceptance of the social order as an order of nature (in contrast to a state of awareness in which *hetero*doxy and *ortho*doxy define each other and conflict). Yet imaginative analysis of worlds alternative to the accepted is universal among

Native Americans. Nor is the analysis prompted by wish fulfillment, a desire to compensate for hardships of a technologically simple existence. An earlier stage of the world is portrayed in myth as rife with dangers and dumbness from which the present, proper world has emerged. Again, a careful reading of myths cannot miss an ingredient of parody of pretension, wealth, and even the central public manifestation of supernatural power, the winter guardian-spirit dance. The mind of man seems everywhere to analyze, and reassemble, something of the fabric of a cultural order, often in the mode of mockery. The naturalization of the cultural of which Bourdieu writes seems always to require an analysis of the nature of the improper, within and without, as Basso suggests. And reflective response to historical disaster, destruction of culture and family security, can be perceived as the motive for recalling and shaping particular myths in particular ways, as with the myths in Clackamas of Victoria Howard, mentioned above. The metalanguage that permits the reflection and response is not one of vocabulary, but of words shaped to dramatic purpose.

Chinookan, and perhaps other Native American myths, can be said to be *abstract calculi of motives* (borrowing a bit from Kenneth Burke's use of the term in two major works [1945, 1950]). There is not much of a vocabulary of motive in Chinookan: some terms ascribing intelligence and stupidity, and the like, and mainly just the polar contrast of the element -*t'u*-, "good, beautiful, valuable, paradigmatic example," and the element -*mla*-, "bad." Yet myth actors are "good to think" (to adapt the phrase of Lévi-Strauss) and in the myths exhibit the consequences of acting in a thoroughgoing way on the basis of particular motives. The outcome of a myth will be fair in relation to a defining actor, according to an implicit matrix whose defining dimensions are maintenance of norms and attentiveness to reality (what Morris Freilich has dubbed *proper and smart*). Implicit in the myths as well are certain values and pervasive exigencies: loyalty to kin, preservation of community, food, and survival. The implications for community give different endings different nuances, as if a chord had been struck, not only a note associated with the defining actor. Variations in endings are variations in the moral to which the narrator has shaped the plot and poetic-rhetorical form.[3]

The terseness of myths, the economy of means in portraits of 'Whiteman', make me think of a comment by Bertrand Russell to the effect that the great virtue of ordinary language was that it could say, for example, *whale,* communicating so much so efficiently with the accuracy required for the occasion. The dramatization of expressive forms, Basso shows us, is efficient in that way. It integrates cognitive and expressive efficiency. Analysis on a page to those who do not share the contextual assumptions has to be long, and part of this book is for that purpose. Yet when we know a portrait in terms of analysis on a page, we do not fully know it. The case is like that of literary translation. A translation must be of a similar scale, amplitude, to have an effect like the original. Better loss of a nuance than two pages to get the nuance right, losing all hope of conveying the original force. The original force was somehow bound up with the original succinctness. It is even more when form is analogous to force. My personal talisman for this is the next-to-last word in a line from Keats's "La Belle Dame Sans Merci": "He set her on his pacing steed." She is almost gone, he with her, before the line reaches the steed.

It seems likewise with the portraits of 'Whiteman'. The dimensions of the portrait are simultaneously analyzed and present. What could be more effective? Such integration seems to me to make the portraits of 'Whiteman' superior for the purposes of the Apache to what analysis alone could hope to be. Many of us know the weakness of learning or teaching or analyzing language, or any facet of culture, apart from experience of its life, of trying to grasp principles apart from embodiments. These portraits have something to say about the unity of theory and practice, the abstract and the concrete.

The portraits are linguistic play, on the one hand, revelation of etiquette, on the other. They should help us to understand how deep are the streams that flow through play and etiquette. Nothing less, in such portraits, than what we owe to each other as fellow human beings, and have a right to expect, as debt and expectation have come to be understood in the experience of the people concerned.

I sense a deep relevance to the nature of art and aesthetic theory as well. I am not competent to develop that relevance. It is just that one cannot help but be stopped by statements such as these:

> Wholly opposed though Adorno and Lukacs are on so many central aesthetic issues, they nonetheless link hands in the assumption that art enables a cognition of essences. . . .

> The comic, for Brecht, comes down to the double-take; it is thus in the first place a formal matter, not a question of "content." But in that question of comic form everything is at stake. . . . Brecht's major achievement is surely to teach us the deep comedy of meta-language . . . (Eagleton, 1978: 31, 32).

There can be no doubt at all of the relevance of these portraits to the response of indigenous peoples the world over to the history of the last several centuries. One autonomous Indian group might enjoy mocking its neighbors in verbal play, and they return the compliment. It is a different matter altogether, of course, to be, not beside, but under, another way of life. There is a considerable literature on the ages of discovery and expansion as to how the rest of the world appeared to the "West." (Much of anthropology, of course, is part of that history, as it became an age of conquest and colonization.) It is not so easy for a Westerner to discover how his kind have appeared to the rest of the world. One may catch a glimpse of Westerners in Japanese genre paintings or the like; the part of the world most involved with anthropology has been surveyed only once in a book, so far as I know (Lips, 1937).

Such forms of expression are often limited to the resistance of caricature and the imaginative righting of scales that in reality remain unfairly weighted. (See, for example, a Clackamas Chinook retort to missionary threats [Howard, 1977: 6]). Such expressive resistance is more likely to be diagnostic of a situation than prognostic of change. It at least testifies that the writ of an alien presentation of self does not run unchallenged, that the hegemony of a bureaucratic order is actively mocked. But such forms of expression may be forerunners of change and need to be considered in that larger context. (The issue is raised by Klein [1966]; cf. Caulfield, 1973: 210, n. 2).

The Western Apache portraits of 'Whiteman' arise circumscribed in occasion and participant, but that may be changed. Certainly their power of analysis, conveyed to a wider world in this book, may change attitudes. And attitude, as the great advocate of dramatistic perspective, Kenneth Burke, has stressed, is incipient act. Until now only Apaches could share these portraits. Now those who sat for them can see them too.

University of Pennsylvania   DELL HYMES
January 1979

References

Basso, Keith. 1970. "To Give Up on Words: Silence in the Western Apache Culture." *Southwestern Journal of Anthropology* 26: 213-30.

 1976. "'Wise Words' of the Western Apache: Metaphor and Semantic Theory." In *Meaning in Anthropology*, pp. 93-122. Ed. K. Basso and H. A. Selby, Jr. Albuquerque: University of New Mexico Press.

Bourdieu, Pierre. 1977. *Outline of a Theory of Practice.* Cambridge: Cambridge University Press.

Burke, Kenneth. 1945. *A Grammar of Motives.* Englewood Cliffs, N.J.: Prentice-Hall. Reprint, 1969. Berkeley: University of California Press.

 1950. *A Rhetoric of Motives.* Englewood Cliffs, N.J.: Prentice-Hall. Reprint, 1969. Berkeley: University of California Press.

Caulfield, Mina Davis. 1973. "Culture and Imperialism: Proposing a New Dialectic." In *Reinventing Anthropology,* pp. 182-212. Ed. Dell Hymes. New York: Random House.

Eagleton, Terry. 1978. "Aesthetics and Politics." *New Left Review* 107: 21-34. (Review of book of this title, edited by Fredric Jameson [London, 1978])

Frachtenberg, Leo J. 1917. "Abnormal Types of Speech in Quileute." *International Journal of American Linguistics* 1: 295-99.

Freilich, Morris. 1975. "Myth, Method, and Madness." *Current Anthropology* 16 (2): 207-26.

Howard, Victoria. 1977. "Five Short Narratives." *Alcheringa* 3: 2-7. Arranged by Charles Bigelow, calligraphed by Kris Holmes.

Hymes, Dell. 1979. "How to Talk Like a Bear in Takelma." *International Journal of American Linguistics* 45 (in press).

Irving, Washington. 1865. *Crayon Miscellany*. The Works of Washington Irving, vol. 6. New York: G. P. Putnam's.

Klein, A. Norman. 1966. "On Revolutionary Violence." *Studies on the Left* 6: 62–82.

Lips, Julius. 1937. *The Savage Hits Back*. New Haven: Yale University Press.

Philips, Susan. 1972. "Participant Structure and Communicative Competence: Warm Springs Children in Community and Classroom." In *Functions of Language in the Classroom*, pp. 370–94. Ed. C. Cazden, V. John, and D. Hymes. New York: Teachers College Press.

1975. "Teasing, Punning and Putting People On." *Working Papers in Sociolinguistics*, no. 28. Austin: Department of Anthropology, University of Texas; Southwestern Educational Research Laboratory.

Sapir, E. 1915. "Abnormal Types of Speech in Nootka." (Canada, Department of Mines, Geological Survey, Memoir 62; Anthropological Series, no. 19). In *Selected Writings of Edward Sapir*, pp. 389–462. Ed. D. G. Mandelbaum. Berkeley: University of California Press.

Williams, W. C. 1954. *The Desert Music and Other Poems*. New York: Random House.

Preface

The fieldwork for this study had its beginnings on July 17, 1965, when, in the Western Apache community of Cibecue, I witnessed a joking imitation of 'the Whiteman' for the first time.[1] For the next ten summers, while also working on other projects, I collected additional joking texts and in close collaboration with Apache consultants from Cibecue started to develop a framework for interpreting them. In the fall of 1975, one of my consultants said to me, "Stop. You've bothered it too much already." So I stopped. Funding for my research was provided by grants from the American Philosophical Society, The Center for the Study of Man (Smithsonian Institution, Washington, D.C.), and the Doris Duke American Indian Oral History Project. Needless to say, I am grateful to these organizations for their support.

The first draft of this essay was written in 1976 while I was a Fellow at the Institute for Advanced Study at Princeton, New Jersey. The final draft was completed during my tenure in 1978 as a Weatherhead Fellow at the School of American Research, Santa Fe, New Mexico. In between, portions of the essay were read at the Institute for Advanced Study; Yale University; Princeton University; the University of New Mexico; and, most recently, at the University of Western Ontario.

I have benefited from the comments and criticisms of many people. To Clifford Geertz, my host for a thoroughly stimulating year at the Institute for Advanced Study, I am indebted for consistently rewarding discussions about ethnography and problems in cultural interpretation. I am also grateful to Thomas Kuhn and Victor Turner, who deepened my understanding of nonostensive semantics and the symbolic structure of ritual drama, respectively. Others have helped in other ways, including Harry Basehart, Richard Bauman, Philip Bock, Harold Conklin, Mac Chapin, Chet Creider, Bill Douglas, James Fernandez, Hildred Geertz, Floyd Lounsbury, Christopher Middleton, Scott Rushforth, David Sapir, Harold Scheffler, David Schneider, Henry Selby, and Joel Sherzer. I am especially mindful of contributions made by Robert Ackerman, Barbara Babcock, Vine Deloria, Jr., Clifford Geertz, Erving Goffman, Ward Goodenough, Philip Greenfeld, John Gumperz, Dell Hymes, Robert Netting, Alfonso Ortiz, and Mary Sanches, all of whom gave close readings to the penultimate draft of the essay and provided specific suggestions for clarifying cloudy points.

Had it not been for Douglas Schwartz, Director of the School of American Research, I do not know when I would have had the opportunity to finish the writing. And to Barbara Babcock, who created an atmosphere in which the writing could get finished, I owe more than I can say. E. W. Jernigan drew the maps and Carol A. Gifford typed the final manuscript, both in expert fashion. My warmest thanks to all; responsibility for errors and shortcomings to none but myself.

The drawings by Vincent Craig that illustrate this essay first appeared in *Fort Apache Scout,* a bimonthly newspaper published by the White Mountain Apache Tribe. For permission to use the drawings here, I wish to thank Mr. Craig and Bill Hess, editor of *Fort Apache Scout.* Mr. Craig, who is a resident of Whiteriver on the Fort Apache Indian Reservation, says with his cartoons many of the things I have tried to say with words. Indeed, he probably says them better.

The symbol used for the type device in this book was created in 1904 by Silas John Edwards, a prominent Western Apache holy man who died recently at the age of 96. The symbol, which Mr. Edwards described as representing "all men, all kinds," is used here with his permission.

For the better part of twenty years, Dell Hymes has played a major role in shaping the aims and methods of linguistic anthropology. Hymes's conception of the field rests on the premise that, in any society, the proper object of inquiry is the full range of communicative functions served by speech, and, therefore, that adequate ethnographic interpretation requires close attention to speaking in all its forms. The present work, which examines one form of speaking in an American Indian society, follows comfortably in this tradition, and thus it is altogether fitting that Hymes should have written the Foreword. His willingness to do so pleased me very much, and I am grateful to him (yet again!) for his kindness and generosity.

Above all, I wish to express my continuing gratitude to the Western Apache of Cibecue who, since 1959, have provided me with friendship, invaluable instruction, and a beautiful place to work. Those people who have served as my consultants know who they are, and it is only because they wish to remain anonymous that I do not mention them by name. Whitemen, Apaches observe, are inclined to say "thank you" so often that the gesture quickly loses significance. I know I run that risk but I have no choice but to take it.

K. H. B.

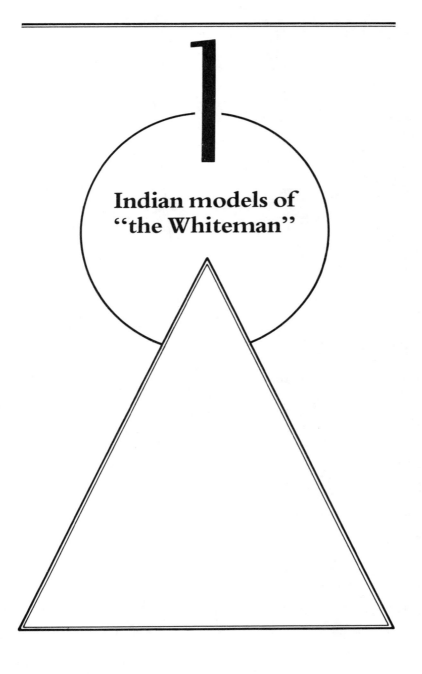

1

Indian models of "the Whiteman"

An Indian, who probably wasn't joking at all, once said, "The biggest of all Indian problems is the whiteman." Who can understand the whiteman? What makes him tick? How does he think and why does he think the way he does? Why does he talk so much? Why does he say one thing and do the opposite? Most important of all, how do you deal with him? Obviously, he is here to stay. Sometimes it seems like a hopeless task.

—Harold Cardinal (*The Unjust Society: The Tragedy of Canada's Indians*)

It has always been a great disappointment to Indian people that the humorous side of Indian life has not been emphasized by professed experts . . . Indians have found a humorous side to nearly every problem and the experiences of life have generally been so well defined through jokes and stories that they have become a thing in themselves . . . The more desperate the problem, the more humor is directed to describe it.

—Vine Deloria, Jr. (*Custer Died for Your Sins: An Indian Manifesto*)

Making sense of other people is never easy, and making sense of how other people make sense can be very difficult indeed. But, as Harold Cardinal observes, it is something that must be done, especially when the welfare of whole societies may be at stake. American Indians have been trying to make sense of Anglo-Americans for a long time, and today, as contact with their "biggest problem" grows increasingly frequent and progressively more intense, the understandings

3

they have reached – their conceptions of who 'the Whiteman' takes himself to be, how he construes his world, why he behaves as he does, and what, in the end, all this reveals about the sort of human creature he is – seem eminently deserving of ethnographic study. This essay is intended as a step in that direction.

Whereas Whitemen are indisputably human beings, American Indian conceptions of 'the Whiteman' are inevitably cultural constructions. And wherever such constructions are found – among the Hopi, the Sioux, or, as in the case I shall discuss here, among the Western Apache – they are invariably drawn in ideal terms. Conforming to no Whiteman in particular, 'the Whiteman' is an abstraction, a complex of ideas and values, a little system of what Alfred Schutz called "taken-for-granted typifications and relevances" that Indian people use to confer order and intelligibility upon their experience with Anglo-Americans.[2] More specifically, 'the Whiteman' may be viewed as an unformalized model: a model *of* Whitemen (in the sense of defining who Whitemen are, how they contrast with other forms of humanity, and what, given these contrasts, they stand for and represent) and a model *for dealing with* Whitemen (in the sense of specifying how Whitemen typically conduct themselves, the circumstances under which particular patterns of behavior are likely to occur, and what, given that one is an Indian, these actions can usually be taken to signify). In short, 'the Whiteman' is a social category and a cultural symbol. It is a multipurpose instrument for rendering Whitemen meaningful.[3]

Although 'the Whiteman' is a prominent symbol in all contemporary American Indian cultures, it should not be assumed that the content of this symbol is everywhere the same. To the contrary, as we shall see, 'The Whiteman' comes in different versions. This diversity arises from the fact that models of 'the Whiteman' are consistently formulated in relation to corresponding models of 'the Indian'. More precisely, it appears to be the case that in all Indian cultures 'the Whiteman' serves as a conspicuous vehicle for conceptions that define and characterize what 'the Indian' is not.[4] And because conceptions of what 'the Indian' *is* vary markedly (obviously, to conceive of oneself as a Western Apache is not the same thing as to conceive of oneself as a Hopi or a Sioux), conceptions of 'the Whiteman' vary as well. In other words, whereas the opposition 'Indian' versus 'Whiteman' is fixed and culturally general, the manner in which this opposition is interpreted is mutable and culturally specific. 'The Whiteman' comes in different versions because 'the Indian' does, and it is just for this reason – that conceptions of the former constitute negative expressions of conceptions of the latter (and vice versa) – that in rendering Whitemen meaningful, 'the Whiteman' renders Indians meaningful as well.

This essay rests on the premise that Indian models of 'the Whiteman' constitute what Clyde Kluckhohn once described as "cultural portraits of ourselves," and that by learning to appreciate these portraits – by analyzing their symbolic content and attending to what they communicate about aspects of the generic *us* – we who are Whitemen can develop a sharper and more sensitive awareness of the impressions we make upon persons whose practices for organizing and interpreting social experience differ from our own.[5] At the same time, and following in the sturdiest of anthropological traditions, we can acquire knowledge of the practices themselves, thus enabling us to speculate about their role in shaping the complicated dilemma with which Mr. Cardinal and other Indian leaders are so justifiably concerned.

And there is a paradoxical bonus: we may also be led to a deeper understanding of American Indian humor and the uses to which humor is put in the management of social relations. For it is by no means uncommon, as Vine Deloria, Jr., has observed, for conceptions of 'the Whiteman' to find articulate expression in jokes. Almost anything can happen in the fictional world of joking, and thus it happens that members of Western Apache communities sometimes step back from the less malleable realm of everyday life and transform themselves into Anglo-Americans through the performance of carefully crafted imitations.[6] On such occasions – when, as Apaches put it, they 'play at being Whitemen' (*indaa' k'ego nadaagołdéhé*) – their conceptions of Anglo-Americans assume uniquely tangible form and become publicly available for everyone, including ethnographers, to witness and evaluate. In the context of joking performances, Western Apache portraits of 'the Whiteman' literally come alive.

The trading post at Cibecue, Arizona – a small, one-room establishment with wide wooden counters, floor-to-ceiling shelves, and a large overhead fan that turns to the rhythm of an earlier and less-hurried time – gets very busy on paydays. And so, on this one a number of years ago, it was understandable that the customers who crowded inside, all of them Western Apaches except myself, paid little attention when another Apache, a man in his early forties, walked in the door and moved to a spot near the rear where one of his cousins, an angular man in his late thirties, was seated on a pile of saddle blankets nursing the remains of a bad cold. Neither did anyone take notice when the two men began to converse in Western Apache, an Athabascan language that has flourished in Cibecue for centuries and that, despite protracted efforts by representatives of the U.S. Government to eradicate it during the present one, survives there today, modified but vigorous, as the standard vehicle for all forms of verbal communication.

Thus, it came as a surprise when the older member of the pair stepped back from his companion, fixed him with a quizzical stare, and broke into a variety of English, proclaiming in a sharp, high-pitched voice, "I don't like it, my friend, you don't look good to me. Maybe you sick, need to eat aspirins!" The effects of this excursion into an alien language (for that, to all but a few Apaches from Cibecue, is just what English is) were instantaneous. Conversation ceased abruptly in other parts of the trading post and everyone turned to see what was happening. "You come to clinic every day, my friend. Sure I help you over there. Sure got lots of aspirins. Maybe you drink too much, that why you sick." As the speaker continued – "You got to sleep, my friend, get lots of sleep" – several bystanders began to smile. And as the monologue reached its climax – "I know all what make you sick, *everything*! So just you don't *forget* it!" – they began to laugh. Moments later, the whole place was in an uproar.

But why? What had been so funny? Smiling weakly, as ethnographers are apt to do when they find themselves confused by something that confuses no one else, I put this question to an Apache standing next to me. "That man," he replied in English, "was just joke his cousin, that's all. He not mad, just saying it, that's all. He was just imitate a Whiteman. Pretty funny, these people think so."

Sociolinguists have observed repeatedly that the languages and language varieties of multilingual speech communities typically exhibit *functional differentiation*. This is a convenient but overly abbreviated way of noting that when

members of such communities engage in verbal interaction
they do not alternate randomly between distinct linguistic
codes but choose systematically among them and put them
to specialized uses (Fishman, 1972; Gumperz, 1976; Hymes,
1974a). There would be nothing remarkable about this if
the occurrence of language alternations were restricted to
situations involving persons whose grammatical competence
in one or more languages was deficient – to situations, that
is, in which code-switching served the purpose of facilitating
or prohibiting intelligible discourse. However, a number of
studies have shown that alternations also occur in situations
whose participants are equally competent in the same set
of languages, and here, where intelligibility is not at issue,
it becomes apparent that code-switching serves other
purposes as well (Gumperz, 1961, 1976; Blom and Gumperz,
1972; Hymes, 1974b; Rubin, 1962, 1968).

In these situations, shifts from one language to another
convey implicit messages about how to construe what is
said, and it is this realization – that code-switching may be
strategically employed as an instrument of metacommunication – that confers upon the matter of functional differentiation a measure of importance. For in helping to clarify
the illocutionary properties of spoken utterances – in
qualifying them as jokes, insults, oaths, or whatever – language alternations also serve to communicate the aims and
sentiments of the persons who perform them, thereby
enabling others to make informed appraisals of what is
going on and, on the basis of these understandings, to
respond in acceptably relevant ways. In short, code-switching
is a linguistic device for framing verbal messages. It is a fine-
grained technique for identifying stretches of talk as particular kinds of doings that are intended to accomplish particular kinds of "work." Consequently, as Jan-Petter Blom and
John Gumperz (1972) have suggested, the *social meanings*
communicated by language shifts may be analyzed as
reflexive statements about the organization of face-to-face
encounters and the structure and content of interpersonal

relationships. Code-switching is an indirect form of social commentary.

When Apaches switch from 'Western Apache' (*indee bi yati'*) to 'English' (*indaa' bi yati'*) for the purpose of imitating Anglo-Americans, they use the language in a special way; and it is this distinctive style of speaking – a style characterized by stock phrases, specific lexical items, recurrent sentence types, and patterned modifications in pitch, volume, tempo, and voice quality – that signals to those familiar with it that a particular form of joking has begun. In addition, the use of this speech style registers information about the joker's immediate surroundings (these have been judged sufficiently informal for joking not to be regarded as inappropriate or tastelessly out of place); the joker's personal identity (he is "fast with words," as Apaches say, and enjoys displaying his verbal skills before an audience); the joker's social identity (he possesses certain statuses that allow him to make temporary play-things of other people); and, most important of all, the joker's relationship with the person who is the object of his joke (their relationship has reached a point where its affective component can be publicly tested and affirmed through the exchange of mock insults). In other words, and this is only to expand on the familiar point made earlier, the social meanings conveyed by acts of code-switching pertain to elements of the situations in which they occur. They are context bound messages that refer indexically to aspects of events currently taking place, and thus may be said to communicate about phenomena that are "present" in the situations themselves.[7]

As the human population of Cibecue has increased during the last decade (today, with slightly more than 1,300

residents, it is the second-largest community on the Fort Apache Indian Reservation), so has the population of cats and dogs. The latter, in particular, are everywhere – lean-bodied, mean-eyed, and ready to quarrel at the smallest provocation. Adult Apaches regard dogs with a mixture of boredom and disdain, but children, who approach the animals fearlessly and cultivate their attentions, take a more hospitable view. This is especially true where puppies are concerned, and so it was, on a day in late August, that a nine-year old girl sat on the ground playing with a lively bundle of fur, which for reasons known only to herself she had decided to name Charles-Bronson. The child's mother was making tortillas in a ramada nearby, and I, sluggish in the heat of the afternoon, was sitting in the shade of a cottonwood tree idly perusing a well-worn copy of the latest catalogue from Montgomery Ward.

Everything was peaceful until the child attempted to pick up the puppy by its tail, an act of abuse to which it responded by yelping loudly and nipping at her hand. Startled but unhurt, she jumped to her feet and glared furiously at the tiny creature. "You're nothing!" she screamed in Western Apache. "You're nothing!" Then, to compound the insult, she slowly turned her back. A few moments later, she faced Charles-Bronson again, but now she was smiling and she addressed the dog in English.

"Bad!" she cried shrilly. "You bad boy! Why you do that – make trouble for me? All time you want make trouble, want fight. You stay here, Charles-Bronson, don't go outside, get punish what you did it. Maybe you going to other classroom. I tell you mother what you did it."

When the girl finished speaking, she reached out for the puppy, but it was not yet ready to be handled and backed away, growling and baring its teeth. At this point, the child's mother intervened. "Stop," she called firmly in Apache, "the dog will bite you again." And then, more sternly, she added, "Be careful how you joke. It's dangerous to imitate a Whiteman."

If it is useful to understand that language alternations convey messages about what is "present" in social situations, it is equally important to recognize that they may convey messages about what is "absent" from them as well. When, for example, a young Apache girl switches codes to joke her puppy in what she takes to be the manner of an Anglo-American schoolteacher scolding a pupil, it is clear that her actions can be interpreted as a statement about her relationship to the dog. On the other hand, and certainly just as clearly, the girl's actions can be interpreted as a statement about the behavior of Anglo-American schoolteachers and their relationship to Western Apache pupils. Indeed, the latter relationship has served as a model for depicting the former. But only the girl and dog are present in the situation. Angry instructors and troublesome students are nowhere to be found.

What has happened, of course, is that the girl has installed herself and her puppy in an imaginary world of play, a world in which their actions are framed in accordance with – and therefore derive their meaning from – a set of cultural premises that pertain to another world on which the imaginary one is patterned (Bateson, 1972; Goffman, 1974). Almost entirely through the use of language, the girl has evoked this primary world to impose a definition upon her own situation. Simultaneously, she has turned a corner of her camp into a classroom, her dog into a rambunctious second grader and, most conspicuous of all, herself into an irate Anglo-American schoolteacher. She has become the leading player in a sociological skit, and, if only for a minute or so, what is nonexistent has become more than a little real.

The capacity of language alternations to frame behavioral acts – and thus, as in the case of Western Apache joking imitations, to invest them with meanings derived from absent orders of reality – is rooted in a process analogous to what analysts of literary style have called *foregrounding* (Garvin, 1969; Gumperz and Hernandez-Chavez, 1971, 1972). This process relies on the fact that the languages of multilingual communities are closely associated with culturally specific attitudes and values that attach to the categories of people who ordinarily speak the languages and the classes of settings and activities in which they are normally spoken. When a language is used in a normal (or unmarked) setting, its cultural associations tend to stay submerged, "inactive," outside immediate awareness. But when the same language is used in an unusual (or marked) setting, these associations become metaphorically high-lighted, or foregrounded, thereby signaling as "relevant now" a particular conceptual framework for understanding what is said and done (Hymes, 1974a). In this way, as Wallace Lambert (1971:95) has observed, "A language switch calls into play contrasting images of the people who habitually speak each of the languages involved"; and it is in terms of these images – or, more exactly, in terms of what they are taken to stand for and represent – that the social meanings conveyed by language alternations are interpreted.

Using slightly different terminology, John Gumperz and Eduardo Hernandez-Chavez (1972:99) have made this same point with respect to alternations among the varieties and styles of single languages.

> Whenever a language variety is associated with a
> particular category of speakers or with certain

april
15

activities, this variety comes to symbolize these features of the non-linguistic environment. In other words, language varieties, like individual words, are potentially meaningful, and in both cases this is brought out by reinterpreting meanings in relation to context. As long as the variety is used in its customary environment, only its basic referential sense is communicated. But when it is used in a new context, it becomes socially marked and the values associated with the original context are mapped onto the new message.

It is important to recognize that when Western Apaches switch linguistic codes to perform joking imitations of *indaa'* ('Whitemen'), they do more than simply call into play a social category and its associated cultural values. In addition, they construct models of this category and stage animated representations of the models. Making use of the distinctive variety of Western Apache English mentioned earlier, as well as of a range of stylized gestures and facial expressions, Apache jokers temporarily transform themselves into mock exemplars of the class of persons whose rightful members their behavior is modeled upon.[8] Thus, they "become" Anglo-Americans, and it is this little miracle – the key element in all successful acts of impersonation – that warrants our attention. For on every occasion that Apaches 'play at being Whitemen', they present concrete formulations of an abstract cultural symbol. The images that they fashion of themselves are images of 'the Whiteman', and the framed world of joking becomes a makeshift studio for an expository form of social portraiture.

This view of Western Apache joking performances – that they are imaginative acts of symbol construction that contain within themselves interpretation of what they are constructions of – bears directly on the fact that portrayals of 'the Whiteman' exhibit a high degree of variability. Western Apache jokers do not produce their imitations by adhering to some fixed and rigid formula. Rather, they mobilize a set of general ideas – their ideas of who White-men are, what they represent, and how they typically behave toward Indians – and adapt them to their own expressive purposes and the fluctuating requirements of particular social occasions. Consequently, though all joking imitations are guided by certain principles, no two imitations are ever the same.[9] Each portrayal of 'the Whiteman' is a novel creation, a personally signed original, a fresh depiction of a familiar subject that is at once a product of its creator's intellect, his mimetic versatility, and the specific inter-personal circumstances that have prompted him to stage an imitation in the first place. In short, every portrayal is unique, and what this implies – obviously perhaps, but significantly nevertheless – is that joking imitations of 'the Whiteman' are more than just symbolic constructions. They are symbolic inventions as well.

On the eastern bank of Cibecue Creek, a narrow river originating in low-lying mountains to the north, there is a large grove of ancient cottonwood trees, and here, on almost any night when the weather is good, Apaches gather to talk, sing, and drink. Before 1963, when selling liquor became legal on the Fort Apache Indian Reservation, the most common drink in Cibecue was *homblu*ˀ ('home brew'), a mild concoction manufactured from malt, brewer's yeast, sugar, and water. But now beer is the favorite – Coors in quart bottles, to be exact – and sometimes it is consumed in large quantities.

This was one such occasion, and the party I joined by the creek was going strong. One man had already fallen asleep, and another, known to us all as a gifted teller of apocryphal tales, was recounting an outrageous adventure in which he, the central character as always, had mistaken a sleeping tarantula spider for a woman's pubis. The situation had been perilous, but our hero, realizing that something was terribly wrong, had finally managed to sort things out correctly and escape without damage – a happy ending to his narrative that was greeted with laughter and loud shouts of approval. Conversation to this point had been conducted exclusively in Western Apache, but suddenly a man I could not see spoke up from the darkness. He was obviously intoxicated and the language he used was English.

"Don't talk dirty that way, my brother. It's no good . . . no good . . . don't do it, my brother. Jesus, pretty soon he gonna get after you, send you some bad place. You read you Bible, my brother. Save you . . . save you . . . save you sinning on Jesus. Hallelujah! Hallelujah! Pretty soon you time gonna come. I know it."

No one spoke, including the storyteller. Then he stood up, a bottle of beer in each hand. "I'm leaving," he said in Western Apache. "I don't like the way someone's joking me." Then he walked off. A few yards away, he turned and shouted back at the top of his voice, "I'm no Christian! Not me!" Shortly thereafter, other people began to leave. The party had come to an end.

I have suggested that Western Apache joking performances may be described and interpreted from at least two perspectives. One of these focuses on the question of how imitations of Anglo-Americans are produced and the kinds of messages they are used to communicate in the context of face-to-face encounters. Here the primary objective is to identify the pragmatic functions served by imitations in the management of interpersonal relations – to discover, in other words, their consequentiality for social actors. The second perspective focuses on the question of what it is that imitations disclose about native conceptions of the classes of persons and activities that are being imitated. Here the basic aim is to identify the interpretive functions of imitations, to analyze them as objectifications of, and figurative statements about, the symbolic content of cultural categories.[10]

This distinction is warranted by the observation that the Western Apache joker always conveys messages about two sets of relationships: (1) a present relationship that currently obtains between himself and the object of his joke, and (2) an absent relationship on which the present one is modeled. What is communicated about the former is inextricably bound up with the joker's personal aims and intentions, and therefore must be analyzed in close conjunction with aspects of the social situation in which the joking encounter takes place. However, what is communicated about the latter can be interpreted without explicit reference to situational features. As Paul Ricoeur (1973) has suggested, messages about absent phenomena may be analytically decoupled from the perishing occasions of their transmission and be treated as *cultural texts* – as what Clifford Geertz (1975b: 448) has neatly described as "stories people tell themselves about themselves," or, turning again to Western Apache joking imitations, as statements by Apaches for Apaches that are about Apaches and the kinds of dealings they have with Anglo-Americans.[11]

Thus, Western Apache joking performances may be said to embody at least two forms of nonreferential meaning. When our concern is with what Apaches employ imitations of Anglo-Americans to express about themselves and their situated relationships with others, we are attending, as noted earlier, to social meanings. On the other hand, when attention is directed to what these imitations express about conceptions of 'the Whiteman' and the relations of Whitemen and Apaches, the terms *cultural meanings* or *textual meanings* can be usefully applied. It goes without saying that this is an analytical separation only, and that social and cultural meanings are no more than different abstractions drawn from single strips of interpersonal activity.[12] In actual joking performances, the two are deeply interfused. Nevertheless, it must be emphasized that appropriate interpretations of social meanings rest upon prior understandings of their cultural counterparts. And this is for a basic reason: the former are always phrased in terms of the latter. In other words, to know what an Apache is saying about his relationship with someone he is joking, one has first to know what he is saying about Anglo-Americans and their relations with Apaches. Conceptions of 'the Whiteman' are primary.

In the remainder of this essay, I shall take a more systematic look at Western Apache joking performances and present a description of some of their social and cultural meanings. Concomitantly, I shall attempt to illustrate a set of informal interpretive procedures – informed in part by recent work in sociolinguistics, in part by an American strain of symbolic anthropology, and in part by the dramaturgical model of human communication developed by Erving Goffman – that I believe may be potentially applicable to imitative acts of all kinds. Primarily, however, I hope to demonstrate the utility of viewing Western Apache joking performances as vehicles for a kind of microsociological analysis that Apaches practice upon themselves and a complex human "problem" whose presence in their lives is a source of pressing concern. Ethnographers, of course, are not the only people who do ethnography, and Western Apache jokers provide an admirable case in point. For in staging imitations of Anglo-Americans, in creating living models of them, Apache jokers give oblique expression to a set of "findings" about them as well. In short, jokers use jokes to make sense of Whitemen, and the questions before us now are how they go about it and what kind of sense they make.[13]

First, however, something more should be said about the community of Cibecue, its connections with Anglo-American communities nearby, and some of the historical circumstances that have shaped Western Apache conceptions of that large group of unknowing subjects who sit for portraits they almost never see.

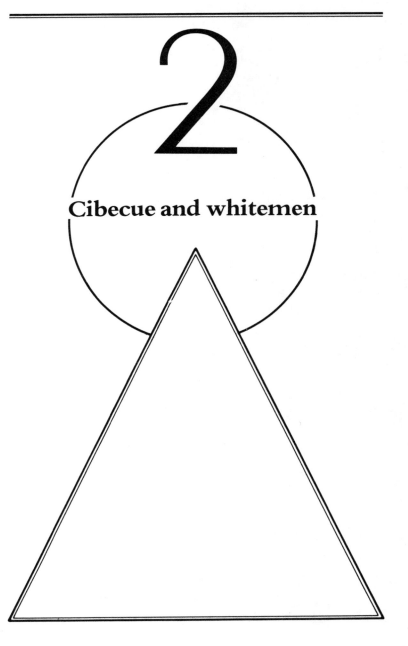

2

Cibecue and whitemen

They came out of nowhere
telling us how to eat our food
how to build our homes
how to plant crops
Need I say more of what they did?

—Soge Track ("Indian Letter,"
Voices from Wah'kon-tah)

The name *Western Apache* is used by ethnologists to designate all those speakers of Southern Athapaskan who lived within the present boundaries of the state of Arizona during historic times, except for the Navajo, the Chiricahua, and a small group of Apaches, known as the Apache Mansos, who resided in the vicinity of Tucson. The population thus delimited, which in 1860 probably amounted to no more than four thousand, was distributed among five regionally distinct subtribal divisions (Goodwin, 1935:55).

The White Mountain Apache, easternmost of the subtribal divisions, ranged over a wide area bounded by the Pinaleño Mountains on the south and the White Mountains on the north. To the southwest, on both sides of the San Pedro River, lived the San Carlos Apache. The territory of a third division, the Cibecue, extended north from the Salt River to well above the Mogollon Rim; its western boundary was marked by the Mazatzal Mountains, homeland of the Southern Tonto. The Northern Tonto, which of all the subtribal divisions lay farthest west, inhabited the upper reaches of the Verde River and ranged north as far as the present town of Flagstaff (see Map 1).

Although the Western Apache engaged in farming, their economy was based primarily on the exploitation of natural resources and the spoils of raiding. Grenville Goodwin, an

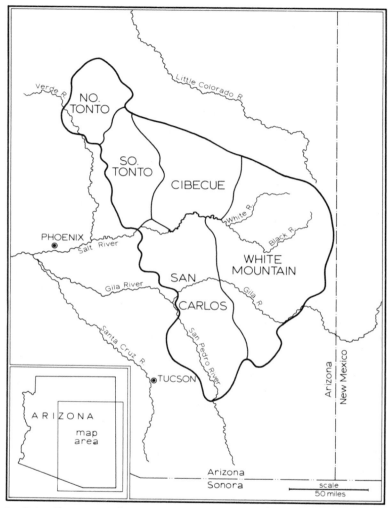

1. Distribution of Western Apache subtribal groups (circa 1850)

ethnographer who worked extensively with the San Carlos Apache in the 1930s, reported that in pre-reservation times agricultural products made up only 25 percent of all the food consumed in a year, the remaining 75 percent being a combination of undomesticated plants, game animals, and stolen livestock (Goodwin, 1937:61). Unable to rely on a surplus of crops, the Western Apache were compelled to travel widely in search of food and, for this reason, did not establish permanent residences in any one place. Indeed, except in the winter months, when plant gathering activities came to a virtual standstill, the people were almost constantly on the move (Goodwin, 1937, 1942).

Each of the Western Apache subtribal divisions was composed of from two to four loosely structured bands. Band distinctions were not as pronounced in some regions as in others, but every band had its own hunting grounds and, except when threatened by starvation, did not encroach upon those of its neighbors. Bands were made up of the most important segments of Western Apache society, what Goodwin referred to as *local groups*. In his words, "these were the basic units around which the social organization, government, and economic activities of the Western Apache revolved" (Goodwin, 1942:110). Local groups varied in size from as few as thirty-five persons to as many as two hundred, but each possessed exclusive rights to certain farming localities, and each was headed by a chief who directed collective enterprises such as raids, hunting expeditions, and dealings with other local groups (Goodwin, 1942). The lack of cohesiveness that characterized Western Apache bands was replaced at the level of the local group by a high degree of unity, mainly because the people who comprised these units were usually related by blood or marriage and were thus obligated to aid each other whenever the need arose (Goodwin, 1942; Kaut, 1957).

When the Gadsden Purchase was ratified in 1853, the

Territory of Arizona came under control of the U.S. Government, and shortly thereafter substantial numbers of Anglo-Americans began to intrude upon the domain of the Western Apache. At first, the Indians were wary but peaceful. However, as soon as it became apparent that the Whitemen intended to claim Apache land and put a stop to Apache raiding into Mexico, apprehension flared into open hostility. The result was a harsh and bitter war that lasted nearly thirty years and ended with the irreversible defeat of the Apache and their consignment to reservations.[14] In 1872 a reservation was created at Fort Apache, this to be the home of the Cibecue people and the northern bands of the White Mountain subtribal division. To the west, Camp Verde became headquarters for the Northern and Southern Tonto. Finally, a large tract of land around Fort San Carlos was set aside for the San Carlos division and the southern White Mountain bands (see Map 2).

As the fighting came to a close, the U.S. Government embarked upon a program designed to prepare the Western Apache for rapid assimilation into Anglo-American society. Three objectives were accorded primary importance (Spicer, 1967). One of these was the economic development of reservations to a point that would provide the Indians with a reliable means of self-support. Another was the opening of schools so that Apache children could be instructed in reading, writing, and "proper etiquette." The third objective was the establishment of churches and the eventual conversion of all Apaches to Christianity.

Over a century after these efforts were begun, it can safely be said that none of them has been wholly successful. Although exploitation of reservation resources has proceeded steadily (lumbering, cattle raising, and tourism are now major tribal industries), many Apaches find themselves victims of poverty (Basso, forthcoming). Practically all Apache children are exposed to English in schools, but

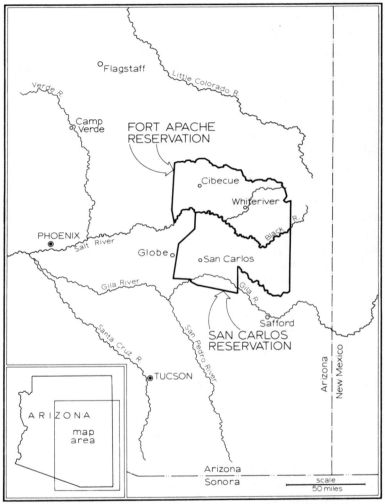

2. Distribution of Western Apache reservations in Arizona (1978)

their first and preferred language is still Western Apache
(Parmee, 1968). And though Christian ministers have made
a number of Apache converts, traditional ritual specialists
(to whom the clergy has always been strongly opposed)
continue to practice their many skills with undiminished
regularity. In short, despite significant steps in the direction
of "modernization," most Western Apaches remain on the
fringe of national American society, maintaining there with
full awareness and quiet satisfaction a cultural system and
a sense of tribal identity that are distinctively and resiliently
their own.

The present community of Cibecue is the most isolated
settlement on the Fort Apache Indian Reservation, a vast
expanse of nearly 1.5 million acres that lies directly north
of the Salt and Black rivers in east-central Arizona. Prior to
1946, when a hastily constructed dirt road established a link
between Cibecue and a state highway fifteen miles away,
access to the village was by wagon track only, and the
Apache who lived there, most of them jobless and dependent
upon horses for transportation, rarely ventured beyond the
boundaries of the reservation. Since then, the road has been
widened and paved, and today, with wage work more common than ever before and pickup trucks as ubiquitous as
horses once were, the residents of Cibecue travel to non-
Indian towns and cities with increasing regularity. Yet as
members of the community are quick to observe, Cibecue
remains a decidedly old-fashioned place where many things
continue to be done in an old-fashioned way. And while
Apaches concede that intensified contact with Anglo-
Americans has precipitated important changes in their
lives, they also point out that in fundamental areas nothing
has changed at all.

Although reservation life has produced far-reaching
modifications in the composition and geographical distribution of Western Apache social groups, consanguineal
kinship, real and imputed, remains the single most powerful

force in the establishment and regulation of interpersonal relationships. The focus of domestic activity is the individual 'camp', or *gowąą*. This term labels both the occupants and the location of a single dwelling or, as is more apt to be the case, of several dwellings located within a few yards of each other. The majority of *gowąą* in Cibecue are occupied by nuclear families. The next largest residential unit is the *gotah* ('camp cluster'), a grouping of spatially localized *gowąą*, each of which has at least one adult member who is related by ties of matrilineal kinship to at least one person living in all the others. An intricate system of exogamous matrilineal clans serves to extend kinship relationships beyond the *gowąą* and *gotah*, thus facilitating concerted action in projects – most notably the presentation of religious ceremonials – that require large amounts of manpower.[15] Despite the presence in Cibecue of a variety of Anglo-American missionaries, diagnostic and curing rituals, as well as the girls' puberty ceremonial, continue to be performed with regularity (Basso, 1970). Belief in witchcraft persists in undiluted form (Basso, 1969).

In the opinion of Apaches, however, Cibecue's conservative character is most clearly reflected in the fact that everyone continues to learn and to speak Western Apache. This is regarded as an achievement of substantial proportions because ever since 1904, when a Lutheran missionary opened a one-room schoolhouse on the bank of Cibecue Creek, Anglo-Americans have made systematic attempts to eliminate the native language and replace it with standard English. The Bureau of Indian Affairs (BIA) established a school at Cibecue in 1933; the Lutherans opened another in 1947; and in 1968, by which time the old Bureau facility had become overcrowded and obsolete, the government constructed yet another. Plainly, it was not from lack of exposure that the people of Cibecue refrained from speaking English.

Right from the start, most Apache parents sent their chil-

dren to school. After all, hot meals were served in the late
fall and winter, clothing was sometimes given away, and
healthy pupils who failed to attend class were hunted down
by truant officers and punished. But right from the start,
Apache parents also instructed their children not to behave
like Whitemen, and, more than anything else, this injunction
applied to the speaking of English. Thus, it is not surprising
that as late as 1934 a teacher at the BIA school in Cibecue
wrote the following in her annual report to the U.S. Com-
missioner of Indian Affairs, Washington, D.C.

> Good discipline has been easily maintained. The
> greatest difficulty encountered is to induce English
> speaking. The Apache language employs the vocal
> organs in a most peculiar manner, and the correct
> pronunciation of English is thus rendered extremely
> difficult. The necessity of the English language is not
> felt, and it is only with great effort, and often by
> stringent measures, that the constant use of the Indian
> language can be held in check (*Report of the Commis-
> sioner of Indian Affairs*, 1934:117).

The next year, in 1935, the same theme was stressed
again.

> The greatest obstacle in the way of progress is the
> aversion of the pupils to the use of the English lan-
> guage. As they but rarely hear any English outside of
> school, they can not be brought to see the need of it,
> and its use can be insured only by disciplinary mea-
> sures. The English used among themselves is so broken
> that a careful observer only can distinguish it from the
> Indian tongue, which is very difficult and guttural (*Re-
> port of the Commissioner of Indian Affairs*, 1935:98).

A great many changes have taken place at Cibecue since
1935, but despite the fact that over 90 percent of the

Apache who live there now control a variety of nonstandard English, they use it only sparingly when conversing with each other. English is reserved almost entirely for encounters with Anglo-Americans and other non-Indians, and in these encounters it is used exclusively. If an Apache from Cibecue wants to buy groceries in Showlow, Arizona, or make a down payment on a pickup truck in Globe, or consult with a physician at the tribal hospital in Whiteriver, or attend a professional sporting event at Phoenix, some knowledge of English is essential. Except for a few missionaries and traders (most of whom are now deceased), Anglo-Americans have never learned to speak Western Apache. Since the end of the so-called Apache wars in 1886, it has always been the other way around.

It is impossible to determine exactly when Apaches living at Cibecue first employed English to perform joking imitations of Anglo-Americans. However, three of the community's oldest members – two women in their eighties and a man over ninety – maintain that it is a fairly recent development dating back no more than forty years. These consultants also concur that the practice was started by schoolchildren, and that for a period of time only young children indulged in it. Just in the last three decades, when face-to-face interaction with Anglo-Americans was becoming a recurrent feature of daily life, did adult Apaches begin to joke in English and cultivate joking imitations into what is recognized today as a full-blown verbal genre. The following account, generously provided by one of the older women I consulted, and translated from the Apache with the help of her bilingual daughter, describes this process in greater detail.

The first time I knew I was a person, people didn't
joke that way. They spoke hardly any English. That
was a long time ago – before 1898, I think. That was

before the Lutherans came over here [1904]. We saw
very few white people around here then. They left us
alone. Later on, more white people came and built
the school out of red stone [1933]. That was when
some children started to joke that way, imitating
white people.

I was married then and had three children. My
oldest son went to the day school. He was seven
or eight years old. One day, he was walking to our
camp with some other boys and my husband got
angry. "Don't be like white people. Don't even joke.
It's no good. Leave it alone!" After that, my son
stopped. But other boys took it up. I used to hear
them sometimes. Many people didn't like it. They
said it sounded bad. They said it didn't sound good.

Grown people didn't joke like that right away.
They waited. Only children did it. Then, one time,
a man living down below tried it. He was drinking
with some people down below when he did it. I
guess he was pretty funny. That's what people said.
I don't know what he did. I only heard about it.
Even so, some people spoke out against him for
joking like that. "Why do you want to act like a
whiteman? Do you wish you could change the color
of your skin?" That's what they said to him. Even
so, some other men started to try it. They were criticized, but I guess they didn't mind it.

The first time I saw a grown person imitate a white
person was when my cousin did it. My husband was off
somewhere and my cousin came to my camp. He was
poor then. He said, "My sister, I'm hungry. I haven't
eaten for two days. Give me some food to eat." After
he finished eating, he was feeling good because he
started joking. He talked like he was a white person,
like he owned a store. He joked at my oldest son.

"Don't steal candy. Don't steal candy." He talked like that.

After the wide road came in here [1946], there were more white people. Some of them wanted to stay away from us. One of them said we smelled like rotten meat. Even so, they acted like they belonged over here. They tried to boss us around. About that time, lots of men started to joke like that, imitating white people. Some of us were afraid. "Don't joke like that," we said. "Some Whiteman will hear about it and get mad." But they did it anyway. Even so, lots of people didn't like it. Some of them still don't like it. They don't like the way it sounds. No good. Some will get mad if someone tries to joke them like that.

That is what happened long ago. I don't know any more. You can have it.

I first became aware that Western Apaches performed joking imitations of Anglo-Americans in 1965, a full nineteen months after I began linguistic and ethnographic research in the community of Cibecue.[16] In part, the tardiness of my discovery can be attributed to the fact that joking imitations are intended to criticize the behavior of Anglo-Americans, and that Apaches, who respond to jokes about themselves with easy equanimity, have serious doubts that Whitemen are comparably good-natured. However, it also reflects the fact that, in comparison to other forms of joking, imitations of Anglo-Americans tend to occur infrequently – so infrequently, in fact, that between 1965 and 1975 I have witnessed only 12 of these performances and gathered reports on only 27 more.

I do not know if this sample is adequately representative of joking imitations performed at Cibecue or at other communities on the Fort Apache Reservation. However, it does provide the basis for a set of empirical generalizations that all of my regular Apache consultants (a group of 8 men and 4 women with whom I have collaborated since 1968) acknowledge as being valid. These may be noted as follows:

1. Joking imitations of Anglo-Americans are usually performed by adult men. (Of the 39 performances in my sample, 35, or 90 percent, were staged by men past the age of thirty.)

2. The objects of joking imitations are usually adult men. (Of the 39 performances in my sample, 32, or 82 percent, were directed at men past the age of thirty.)

3. Joking imitations are not restricted to persons who stand to each other in a particular kinship relationship. This includes relationships such as 'matrilateral cross-cousin' (*shi biłna'aash*) and 'sibling-in-law' (*shiyį*) in which some amount of joking is obligatory. (Of the 39 performances in my sample, 17, or 44 percent, were directed at members of the joker's own clan; 8, or 20 percent, at members of the joker's father's clan; 4, or 10 percent, at members of the joker's wife's clan; and 10, or 26 percent, at persons to whom the joker was unrelated by either clan or marriage.)

4. Joking imitations are frequently performed in the context of 'drinking parties' (*'iidląą'*), a social activity that typically involves at least half a dozen participants, sometimes many more. (Of the 39 performances in my sample, 28, or 72 percent, were staged by men who were drinking with friends and relatives at the time.)

This last observation should not be taken to mean that Apaches who perform joking imitations of Anglo-Americans are likely to be intoxicated. To the contrary, as several of my consultants pointed out, successful joking imitations require a kind of mental and verbal dexterity that drunkenness temporarily destroys. It is significant, however, that jokers are said to be at their best when they are "feeling good," a condition stimulated in equal measure by the lively company of other people and small amounts of alcohol. Under these circumstances, Apaches say, reticence disappears and jokers are moved to exercise their skills with an enthusiastic lack of restraint that makes their performances all the more amusing. One of my consultants put it this way:

Some men only joke like Whitemen when they been drinking. They do it best that way. They don't get drunk, just drink a little – maybe just one, two cans. That way, they really want to work on it – so it's real funny. Some are too shy, so that's why they drink a little. It makes them happy. That way, it's easy for them to joke. They can do it real good – makes everybody laugh.

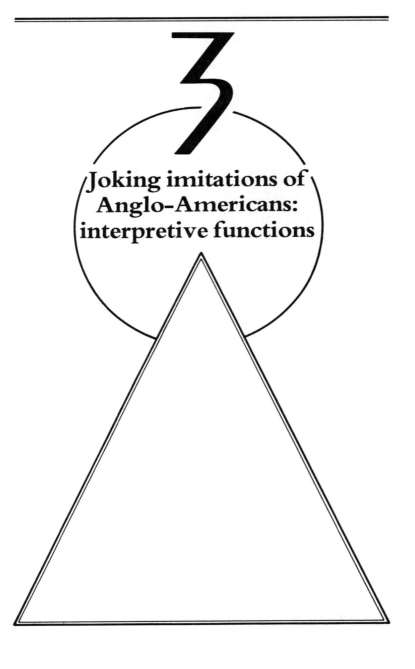

3

Joking imitations of Anglo-Americans: interpretive functions

What the white man doesn't realize is the tenacity of Indians. They simply don't realize the utter individuality of Indian people and their belief in one thing more than absolutely anything else: being Indian.

—Fritz Scholder (Interview, *Song from the Earth: American Indian Painting*)

My interpretation of Western Apache joking imitations proceeds on the twin assumptions that joking is a form of play, and that play is characterized by a paradox of the Russellian, or Epimenides, type, consisting in a negative statement that contains within it an implicit negative metastatement (Bateson, 1972). Accordingly, acts of play may be defined as those which are modeled on acts that are "not play," but which are understood not to communicate what would be communicated by these acts if they were performed unplayfully.[17] So it is with joking. Acts of joking convey messages that are not conveyed when the acts they are patterned after are performed unjokingly, and for this reason jokes are not intended to be taken literally, "seriously," or at face value (Austin, 1962:121). In the event that they are, they instantly cease being jokes and, having thus gone awry, stand open to interpretation as instances of the unjoking acts they are modeled upon. The social consequences of such interpretations may be sharply disruptive, for the acts that jokes most closely resemble – the acts they are patterned after but are not intended to be – are slurs, criticisms, and insults (Radcliffe-Brown, 1940; Labov, 1972). Western Apaches express their own understanding of these conditions by observing that jokes are simultaneously 'funny' (*dabagodlohé*) and 'dan-

37

gerous' (*benagodzig'*). In order to appreciate what is meant
by this assertion – and why, more specifically, Apaches
maintain that it applies with particularly telling force to
joking imitations of Anglo-Americans – we must look again
at the manner in which these imitations are performed and
consider more closely the kinds of transformations they
entail.

Jokes classified as *banagozdí'* by the Western Apache
are distinguished from all other forms of 'humorous speech'
(*dabagodlohé yałti'*) by a single defining attribute: the
person at whom the joke is directed is depicted as something he or she is not. In other words, the object of the
joke, whom I shall hereafter refer to as the butt, is made
the subject in a metaphor.[18] There seem to be three ways
in which this can be accomplished. In the first and simplest
case, illustrated in (1) below, the joker likens the butt to
a class of material objects.[19]

1. *Setting:* A hunting camp twenty miles north of Cibecue.
   Participants: Six Apache men, including A (age 31) and B
   (age 27), and KHB.
   Scene: It is late at night and the men are preparing to go
   to sleep. B is standing near a small fire warming himself,
   and A, seated on his bedroll close by, is drinking coffee.
   A: Are you sleepy?
   B: Yes. It's cold, isn't it? I brought only one blanket
   with me.
   A: I guess your rifle case will be warm enough.
   [At this point, several of the men, including B, laugh
   softly.]
   B: So! I'll shoot deer with myself.
   Note: B is unusually tall for a Western Apache (well over
   six feet) and is also very thin.

A second technique for accomplishing *banagozdí'*,
exemplified in (2), is for the joker to metaphorically place

the butt in a social category to which he or she does not rightfully belong, typically in reference to a third party who is absent from the scene.

2. *Setting:* A footpath in Cibecue.
   Participants: Two Apache men (C, age 45, and D, age 42) and KHB.
   Scene: C and D meet on the trail and stop to talk.
   C: Where are you going?
   D: Across the creek.
   C: So! You're looking for your wife, E, are you?
   D: [Smiling] She left me three days ago, and now I'm lonely and hungry.
   C: I knew it!
   Note: E is not D's wife. D has been married to the same woman for eighteen years. E is an attractive, high-spirited widow whose enthusiasm for lovemaking is legendary, whose skills in this area are said to be highly refined, and whose fondness for recounting her adventures in explicit detail produces in the men of Cibecue a mixture of fear and amazement that borders on genuine awe.

In the third and most-complex form of *banagozdi'*, the joker places *himself* in a social category to which he does not belong, and, by acting as if his membership in that category were valid, proceeds to locate the butt in another category, equally fictitious, that is associated with the first. This is nicely illustrated by the joking encounter reported in (3) where an Apache man lays claim to being a 'ceremonial speaker' (*gojitaał yadiłti'*) and then lectures his ex-wife's sister as though she were one of his charges.

3. *Setting:* A ceremonial dance ground in Cibecue at which a curing ritual is in progress.
   Participants: F, an Apache man (age 55+); G, his ex-sister-in-law (age 50+); and KHB.

Scene: Western Apaches from several communities on
the Fort Apache Reservation have come to take part in
the ceremonial, and F, who is a resident of Cibecue, has
just greeted G, who lives with her husband and children
in Whiteriver. Both F and G have been drinking beer and
are feeling ebullient.

F: So! You've come here to dance, have you?

G: Yes! I've come to enjoy myself and have a good time.

F: You better act properly like everyone else. Don't
drink too much! I'm the speaker here. I don't want
any trouble. I want you to think right. It's no good
when unmarried girls chase after men. It's no good.
When unmarried girls chase after men, the people
don't like it. They will talk badly about you. I know
you like to chase after men. Listen to what I'm
telling you. Your mother should be watching you.
I want you to stay close to the fire so I can watch
you. Don't try to sneak off!

G: [Laughing] So you'll be watching me, will you?

F: [Laughing] Yes!

Note: F is not and has never been a ceremonial speaker.
G is not and has never been sexually promiscuous.

Jokes accomplished in this fashion warrant attention
on several counts. To begin with, the essential means by
which the joker announces his joking identity is by speaking
in a way that foregrounds the status-role category with
which that identity is culturally associated. In (3), for
example, the joker, F, proclaims his identity as ceremonial
speaker by switching linguistic codes and parodying a
marked speech style called *gozhǫǫ yałtiʔ* ('good words',
'beneficial words') that bona fide members of this category
employ to deliver short orations before the start of ritual
events. Concomitantly, the joker confers a joking identity
upon the butt, imputing to the latter membership in a status-

role category that is structurally implicated by the foregrounded category in which the joker has placed himself.
Thus, again in (3), F confers upon G the identity of *'ich'ikii*
('unmarried girl') which, being one of several linked to
gojitaal yadiłti' ('ceremonial speaker'), provides him with
a warranted pretext for depicting her as an adolescent. In
this way, then, a metaphor is joined and the parameters of
a joking relationship are defined. A double transformation
has taken place, and it is in terms of the joking identities
thus established that interaction now proceeds. The joker
has authored a tiny world of make-believe and has set the
stage for a comparably diminutive drama in which he and
the butt will be the leading players.

Imaginative though it is, this little drama is not entirely
a product of the joker's imagination. As mentioned earlier,
the scene he stages and the characters he animates are
patterned on slices of unjoking activity that he employs
in the capacity of a model, or what I propose to call a
primary text. Drawn from various sectors of community
life, these strips of "serious" behavior furnish the raw
materials from which joking performances are fashioned.
Consequently, any actual performance may be said to
consist in the construction and presentation of a *secondary
text* that is intended to be understood as a facsimile or
transcripted copy of the primary text on which it is patterned.[20] This, of course, is not made explicit by the
joker because the success of his performance – how well it
"comes off" – depends upon his ability to persuade the butt
to play along, that is, to pretend with him that the facsimile he has constructed is not a facsimile, that the secondary text is a primary one, and that the whole affair
is not a mock-up of some precedent reality, but that reality
itself. In other words, the joker invites the butt to sustain
a sociological fiction, and for a few seconds, or however
long it may be until the joke comes to an end, they share

together in a familiar but nonetheless illusionary world – a world in which genial old men become ceremonial speakers, where respectable women become juvenile flirts, and where, as we shall see before long, Western Apaches become 'Whitemen'.

Within this world of counterfeit characters and simulated social encounters, the Apache joker is able to take moral liberties he cannot take outside it. In the first place, he can toy with the butt, deliberately making of him or her a temporary plaything, a passive object for the amusement of others. In addition, he can openly ascribe to the butt a set of personal and social characteristics that the latter does not possess – characteristics, it should be emphasized, that are consistently unflattering and frequently downright defamatory. Finally, and most obviously, the joker can exploit his own and the butt's joking identities, using these fabrications as an excuse to behave in ways which, if the joking frame were not firmly fixed in place, the butt and others would be obligated to regard as a deliberate attempt at public humiliation. In short, the world of joking provides moral cover for immoral social acts. It is a rough-and-tumble playground in which Apaches can violate cultural norms and avoid the consequences such violations normally entail.

By way of illustration, consider again the joking encounter described in (3) above. The butt, G, is a wife and mother of some thirty years, a shaman with two minor ceremonials, and a person who places considerable stock in appearances. Then there is F, a man with a scandal or two in his past, who has had trouble keeping wives, and who, at present, living with an older sister who wishes he would move on, is a bit too given over to beer and wine. Now, for a stalwart like this to address a pillar of society as if she were a hot-blooded teenager bent upon running off somewhere for the sole purpose of having sexual intercourse – well, such a thing would be unthinkable outside the confines of a joke. Not only would F be open to strenuous criticism from all sides, but, since G controls supernatural power, he would also have to worry about the possibility of retaliation in the form of witchcraft. But F is an accomplished joker, the fiction he created was effectively sustained, and no one wondered for a moment about what might have happened if G had refused to play along. Sometimes, however, the butts of jokes do not play along, and when this happens – when secondary texts are read as primary ones and the joking frame "breaks" – the consequences can be explosive. This is why Apaches say that joking is 'dangerous' (*benagodzig?*).

Jokes involving imitations of Anglo-Americans are said to be among the most dangerous of all. Paradoxically, however, and therefore not inconsistently, they are also considered extremely 'funny' (*dabagodlohé*). Why should this be so? Like ceremonial speakers, maternal uncles, trading-post clerks, and all the other figures that find their way into Apache jokes, Anglo-Americans are not intrinsically amusing. They are made to seem that way by the persons who imitate them. How, then, are these imitations accomplished? What does the joker do that makes 'the Whiteman' so laughable? First of all, as we have seen, the joker animates a character. But more than this is involved – he *portrays* a character as well. Although the joker works from bits and pieces of actual experience, these comprising what I have called a primary text, he is free to build upon this experience and depart from it in various directions. Accordingly, he can stage his character in different settings, present him in different lights, and imbue him with different qualities of attitude, temperament, and demeanor. In short, the joker can be interpretive and inventive. But for all this flexibility of expression (a flexibility, incidentally, that sometimes imparts to joking imitations the illusory appearance of unregulated outbursts), the joker goes about his business in conformity with very definite procedures. It is to these procedures – the principles for constructing secondary texts from primary ones – that I now wish to direct attention.

Western Apache jokers pursue invention and interpretation through caricature and hyperbole, portraying their characters so as to make them appear ludicrous and ridiculous.[21] These effects are achieved in accordance with a single overarching strategy – I shall call it *epitomization* – that is informed and guided by two major principles: *contrast* and *distortion*. These principles operate on the content and form of behavioral acts, respectively, and specify two sets of conditions: (1) which elements of Anglo-American behavior are to be selected for imitation, and (2) how the selected elements are to be presented and displayed. Each principle is composed of a set of subprinciples, or rules, which may be stated as follows.[22]

I. CONTRAST PRINCIPLE

A. Choose for imitation the members of a status-role category typically occupied by Anglo-Americans (e.g., *izee? nant?án*; 'physician') that is culturally paired with a second category typically occupied by Western Apaches (e.g., *?an hindii*; 'patient').

B. Using the joking variety of Western Apache English mentioned earlier (see also II.a.1 below), foreground the status-role category chosen in I.a with stock phrases (e.g., *"How you feeling?"*) and lexical items (e.g., *aspirin*) that are associated with forms of activity in which members of the first category regularly engage with members of the second category (e.g., a medical interview).

C. Select for presentation elements of Anglo-American behavior (congruent with, but not necessarily limited to,

the status-role categories and activities foregrounded in
I.b) that contrast with functionally equivalent elements
in the behavioral repertoire of Western Apaches.

II. DISTORTION PRINCIPLE

A. Distort the behavioral elements selected in I.c by modify-
ing aspects of their form, thereby heightening the contrasts that motivated their selection in the first place.

  A.1. With regard to elements of verbal behavior, distortion may be accomplished in one or more of the
following ways: (1) increased speech volume; (2)
increased speech tempo; (3) exaggerated elevations in
pitch; (4) repetition of whole phrases; (5) modifications in voice quality (chiefly by means of glottal
constriction combined with heavy nasalization of
vowel segments) so as to achieve the effect of
stridency.[23]

  A.2. With regard to elements of nonverbal behavior,
distortion may be accomplished in one or more of the
following ways: (1) exaggerated abruptness or jerkiness
of movement; (2) repetition of movements; (3) length-
ened duration of visual and bodily contact.

The comic effects produced by the application of these
principles cannot be properly appreciated unless the cultural
contrasts they are used to highlight are made explicit. Therefore, I should now like to consider the text of a single,
unusually long joking performance in which a number of
these contrasts are exemplified with particular clarity and
force.[24] Staged by one of the most practiced jokers from
Cibecue, this performance depicts 'the Whiteman' in the
role of 'bar owner' (*bía bana? idíʾhi*) and the butt in the
role of an Apache 'customer' (*bía ?iidląą? na?iłdii*). It is
an excellent example of the joker's craft.

4. *Setting:* The living room of an Apache home at Cibecue.
  Participants: J, a cowboy (age 40+); K, his wife (age 37);

four of their children (ages 4–12); L, a clan 'brother' of J (age 35+).

Scene: It is a hot, clear evening in mid-July, and J and K have just finished a meal. J is seated on a chair, repairing a bridle. K is washing dishes. Their children play quietly on the floor. L is not yet present.

J: *ʔiskąą dohwasitʔaago goʔąąda.* (I'll be away all day tomorrow'.)

K: *haayó makashi nanałtseʔ* ('Where are the cattle'?)

J: *goshtlʔísh bitoo bishaayó nanałtseʔ* ('They're near Mud Springs',)

K: *ʔaa.* ('Yes',)

[J starts to speak again but is interrupted by a knock on the door. He rises, answers the knock, and finds L standing outside.]

J: Hello, my friend! How you doing? How you feeling, L? You feeling good?

[J now turns in the direction of K and addresses her.]

J: Look who here, everybody! Look who just come in. Sure, it's my Indian friend, L. Pretty good all right!

[J slaps L on the shoulder and, looking him directly in the eyes, seizes his hand and pumps it wildly up and down.]

J: Come right in, my friend! Don't stay outside in the rain. Better you come in right now.

[J now drapes his arm around L's shoulder and moves him in the direction of a chair.]

J: Sit down! Sit right down! Take your loads off you ass. You hungry? You want some beer? Maybe you want some wine? You want crackers? Bread? You want some sandwich? How 'bout it? You hungry? I don't know. Maybe you get sick. Maybe you don't eat again long time.

[K has stopped washing dishes and is looking on with amusement. L has seated himself and has a look of bemused resignation on his face.]

J: You sure looking good to me, L. You looking pretty
     fat! Pretty good all right! You got new boots? Where
     you buy them? Sure pretty good boots! I glad . . .
[At this point, J breaks into laughter. K joins in. L shakes
his head and smiles. The joke is over.]
K: *indaaˀ dogoyą́ą́da*! ('Whitemen are stupid'!)

Before proceeding further, let us take note of an observation made by the literary critic Alfred Kazin (1972:220).

A person is seen to be ludicrous when the manner in
which he does something contrasts so strikingly with
how that something should be done, or is normally
done, that he appears totally and hopelessly incompetent. One sees this clearly when Chaplin stirs a pot of
stew with his shoe, or bathes in a tub without water,
or tips his hat in greeting to a horse.

Acts such as these seem ludicrous because they are perceived to be flagrantly "wrong," suggesting that something
is comparably wrong with the persons who perform them.
What is wrong with these persons is that they apparently
lack the knowledge and ability to do even the simplest
things "right," and, as any circus-goer will readily attest,
individuals who display this fundamental form of incompetence can be very funny indeed. Commenting on Henri
Bergson's famous essay on laughter, Erving Goffman (1974:
38) makes the same point in a more useful way.

In pointing out that individuals often laugh when
confronted by a person who does not sustain in every
way an image of human guidedness, Bergson only
fails to go on and draw the implied conclusion, namely,
that if individuals are ready to laugh during occurrences
of ineffectively guided behavior, then all along they
apparently must have been fully assessing the con-
formance of the normally behaved, finding it to be no
laughing matter.

When Western Apaches stage joking imitations of Anglo-Americans, they portray them as gross incompetents in the conduct of social relations. Judged according to Apache standards for what is normal and "right," the joker's actions are intended to seem extremely peculiar and altogether "wrong." In other words, the image the joker presents of 'the Whiteman' is an image of ineffectively guided behavior, of social action gone haywire, of an individual stunningly ignorant of how to comport himself appropriately in public situations.[25] To see more precisely how the behavior of the joker's 'Whiteman' conflicts with Apache expectations, let us return to the joking performance recorded in (4) and examine it piece by piece.

1. *Hello, my friend!* Throughout J's performance, he addresses L as "my friend," an expression that Apaches think Anglo-Americans bandy about in a thoroughly irresponsible way. There is no word in Western Apache that correspondends precisely to the English lexeme *friend*. The nearest equivalent is *shich ʾinzhoni* ('toward me, he is good'), an expression used only by individuals who have known each other for many years and, on the basis of this experience, have developed strong feelings of mutual confidence and respect. In contrast, Apaches note, Anglo-Americans refer to and address as "friends" persons they have scarcely met, persisting in this practice even when it is evident from other things they say and do that they hold these individuals in low esteem. More specifically, Whitemen are said to make liberal use of the term when they want something from someone, apparently believing that by professing affection and concern they can improve their chances of getting it. In short, Anglo-Americans pretend to what cannot and should not be pretended to – hasty friendship – and it strikes Apaches as the height of folly and presumptuousness that they do. One of my consultants put it succinctly: "Whitemen say you're their friend like it was nothing, like it was air."

2. *How you doing? How you feeling, L? You feeling good?* Except among persons who enjoy close relations, such as husbands and wives, unsolicited queries concerning an individual's health or emotional state constitute impertinent violations of personal privacy. If an Apache wishes to discuss such matters, he or she will do so. If not, they are simply nobody's business. But Anglo-Americans make them their business, and they go about it with a dulling regularity that belies what Apaches consider an unnatural curiosity about the inner feelings of other people. This is interpreted as a form of self-indulgence that in turn reflects a disquieting lack of self-control – the same lack of control, Apaches say, that manifests itself in the prying queries of

young children and the unrestrained babblings of old
people afflicted with senility.

3. *Look who here, everybody! Look who just come in.
Sure, it's my Indian friend, L. Pretty good all right!* When
an Apache joins or leaves a social grouping, he or she
prefers to go about it unobtrusively, for there are occasions
on which it can be embarrassing to have public attention
called to one's comings and goings. Anglo-Americans, on
the other hand, typically acknowledge such events with
what Apaches regard as a great deal of fuss and unnecessary
fanfare, causing the person who is the object of it to feel
momentarily isolated and socially exposed in a way that
can be acutely uncomfortable. Such commotions contain
a humorous element because they impress Apaches as being
completely gratuitous. What could be more readily apparent, they ask, than the fact of someone's arrival at the
scene of a social gathering? Children may delight in calling
attention to the obvious. But adults?

4. On three separate occasions, J addresses L by his
name. 'Personal names' (*ʔizhiʔ*) are classified by the Western
Apache as items of 'individually owned property' (*shiyéé*).
Consequently, calling someone by name is sometimes
likened to temporarily borrowing a valued possession. The
metaphor is apt, for just as rights of borrowing imply
friendship and solidarity, so do rights of naming, and
therefore the use of personal names in direct address is
understood by Apaches to serve as a marker of social
relationships characterized by trust and goodwill. But the
right to name must be exercised judiciously because persons
who name too much, like persons who borrow too often,
can be justly accused of engaging in an obsequious form of
exploitation that violates the rights of others. For this
reason, even among individuals who have established close
relationships, name avoidance is the rule rather than the
exception. In contrast, Apaches point out, Anglo-Americans

think nothing of using a person's name as soon as they learn it, a practice that arises from the same lack of understanding that leads them to the premature use of expressions such as "my friend." More astonishing still, Whitemen are observed to use the same name over and over again in the same conversation. This practice is harder to understand. A frequent explanation, only slightly facetious, is that Whitemen are exceedingly forgetful and therefore must continuously remind themselves of whom they are talking to.

5. J slaps L on the back, shakes his hand repeatedly, looks him squarely in the face, and, having grasped him around the shoulder, guides him to a seat. Except when participating in activities that necessarily involve physical contact, Western Apaches are careful to avoid touching each other in public. This is especially true of adult men. Back-slapping and vigorous handshaking are regarded as direct and unwarranted encroachments upon the private territory of the self. Similarly, any form of touching that lingers without apparent reason can provide grounds for suspicion because of its homosexual overtones. Prolonged eye contact, especially at close quarters, is typically interpreted as an act of aggression, a display of challenge and defiance. And if Apaches were ever to engage in the kind of forcible "steering" that J inflicts upon L when he maneuvers him to a seat, this would be seen as an open violation of the individual's right to freedom of movement. Needless to say, Anglo-Americans take a different view of the social uses and social significance of visual and bodily contact. By Apache standards, Whitemen are entirely too probing with their eyes and hands, a distasteful tendency that Apaches take to be indicative of a weakly developed capacity for self-restraint and an insolent disregard for the physical integrity of others. As one of my consultants put it: "Whitemen touch each other like they were dogs."

6. *Come right in, my friend! Don't stay outside in the*

rain. Better you come in right now. Sit down! Sit right down! Take your loads off you ass. These utterances are directives in the imperative mode, and it is precisely on this account – that they entail "bossing someone around" – that Apaches find them offensive. If a visitor to an Apache home wants to enter it and sit down, he will quietly ask permission, wait until it is given, and then find an unoccupied space within. If not, he will state his business at the door, conduct it there or at a short distance away, and depart after a requisite exchange of pleasantries. To insist that the visitor come inside, to command him, is to overrule his right to do as he chooses, thereby implying that he is a person of little account whose wishes can be safely ignored. "When you talk to people like this," one of my consultants said, "you run over them. You make them feel small." To avoid such displays of disrespect, Apaches either refrain from issuing directives or construct them in ways so circumlocutional and oblique that they typically carry the force of observations rather than others. (An example: *łąą tsįyaané dijįį?*, 'There are lots of mosquitoes today', is equivalent to "Don't go hunting without a jacket.") In contrast, many of the directives employed by Anglo-Americans impress Apaches as being extremely blunt and unduly harsh, their coercive impact far exceeding what Apaches consider necessary to accomplish their often trivial purposes. Said one of my consultants:

> Even it's something little – like they want you to
> close the door – even for something like that, some
> Whiteman talk like they bossing you around. It's like
> shooting rabbits with a .30-.30.

7. *You hungry? You want some beer? Maybe you want wine? You want crackers? Bread? You want some sandwich? How 'bout it? You hungry?* Except in times of emergency, Apaches consider it rude to repeat a question more than

once or twice. Similarly, because everyone is accorded the right to take plenty of time before speaking, it is also considered discourteous to request or demand replies. Under normally relaxed circumstances, rapid-fire questioning of the kind J engages in is regarded as an act of coercion, a type of verbal strong-arming aimed at extracting information by creating an atmosphere of urgency in which the individual at whom it is directed feels pressured to respond. Consequently, it can also be interpreted as an expression of anger and irritation. Apaches agree that Anglo-Americans are inclined to ask too many questions and to repeat the same question (or minor variants of it) too many times. This gives them the appearance of being in a state of extreme hurry and aggravated agitation, which, besides being distinctly unattractive, sometimes causes them to lose sight of what Apaches take to be an obvious and important truth: carefully considered replies to questions are invariably more reliable (because less likely to be retracted or modified) than replies that have been rushed.

8. *I don't know. Maybe you get sick. Maybe you don't eat again long time.* Most Western Apaches hold firmly to the understanding that talking about trouble and adversity can increase the chances of its occurrence. Consequently, when speaking about themselves or others, they avoid making statements that suggest or allude to the possibility of misfortune, especially sickness and death. In contradistinction, Anglo-Americans are observed to speak about such matters often and in what Apaches regard as a supremely casual fashion, a practice that gives rise to the bizarre impression that Whitemen are eager to experience hardship and disaster.

9. *You sure looking good to me, L. You looking pretty fat! Pretty good all right! You got new boots? Where you buy them? Sure pretty good boots!* Like unsolicited queries about one's health or emotional state, remarks concerning

one's physical appearance are criticized by Apaches. What is wrongly involved, they explain, is being publicly 'noticed' (-*ish ʾií ʾ*) in a manner that focuses attention on aspects of one's private person. This can be a source of discomfort because it means that one has been the subject of a close but covert examination, and that something – added weight, an item of clothing, a cut or bruise – has been found wanting or out of the ordinary. As a result, the individual is forced to take notice of himself and is made to wonder if he 'stands out' (-*naijaa ʾ*), a form of self-consciousness to which Apaches are keenly sensitive and therefore are anxious to avoid. By comparison, Anglo-Americans do not seem to mind standing out, or causing others to stand out, at all. On the contrary, given the amount of time they spend talking about their hair, faces, bodies, and dress, they appear to enjoy it immensely. The conclusion Apaches draw from this is that Whitemen are deeply absorbed with the surfaces of themselves, an obsession that stems from a powerful need to be publicly perused and to be regarded as separate and distinct from other people. Said one of my consultants:

> Whitemen can look each other over. They do it all the time. They don't care about it. They try to look different all the time. Some change clothes every day. Some don't wear shirt. Some just wear real old, dirty clothes. Same way it is with women. Some don't wear much so you can see their bodies. We don't like it that way, so we stay away from it. We don't talk about it – how somebody's look. Even he's real poor, or losing weight, or hurt bad with something showing [i.e., a cast or bandage]. You do that and he's going to get mad at you. He thinks you looking him over – like he's some cattle in a corral.

10. Throughout J's performance, he speaks rapidly in a

loud, high-pitched voice. In ordinary conversation, Apaches address each other in low, softly modulated tones and at a pace they consider measured and deliberate. By comparison, they say, they are forcefully struck by the speech of Anglo-Americans, which is regularly described as being too fast, too loud, and too 'tense' (*ndǫ́ǫ́*; a commonly drawn analogy is with a muscle stretched to the point of pain). Among themselves, Apaches associate these suprasegmental phenomena with the expression of criticism and indignant self-assertion – with the voice of a woman scolding a child, for example, or with that of a man responding to an insult. As a result, Anglo-Americans, even when speaking in a manner that they consider genial and relaxed, may easily give the impression of being vexed and irate. Most Apaches recognize this disjunction and on occasions find it amusing, as when they observe, "Whitemen are angry even when they're friendly." But there are also times when they find it unsettling and slightly menacing. One of my consultants commented as follows:

> Whitemen make lots of noise. With some who talk like
> that – loud like that and tight – it sounds too much
> like they mad at you. With some, you just can't be
> sure about it, so you just got to be careful with them
> all the time.

And so it goes – joke after joke, year after year – the joker's 'Whiteman' rattling on at breakneck speed while the butt's 'Apache', silent and composed, attempts to make sense of the outlandish character that has materialized before him. This is not difficult, and the butts of jokes usually express their reactions succinctly. "Whitemen are stupid!" K proclaims at the conclusion of J's performance. As far as Apaches are concerned, nothing more is necessary. Laughter says the rest.

Enough has been said, I think, to demonstrate that contrast and distortion lie at the heart of Western Apache joking performances.[26] By the same token, it should now be apparent that the cultural or textual meanings of these performances – the messages they communicate about Whitemen and Western Apaches, and how Whitemen and Apaches get along together – are intimately bound up with significant differences that Apaches perceive between their own practices for accomplishing social interaction and practices employed by Anglo-Americans. Indeed, these differences and the discordancies they produce in face-to-face encounters comprise the fundamental subject matter of secondary texts, and it is for this reason that the scenes jokers stage – scenes in which Western Apaches invariably get "run over" by Whitemen – are properly interpreted as dramatized denunciations of the ways in which Anglo-Americans conduct themselves in the presence of Indian People.

Let us examine this proposition in greater detail. As we have seen, the immediate effect of joking imitations is to place two versions of human guidedness in sharp juxtaposition. The Anglo-American version, of course, is represented by the joker and finds overt expression in the exaggerated actions of 'the Whiteman' he has temporarily become. The Western Apache version is represented by the butt and remains implicit, providing the conceptual equipment – the categories, values, and assumptions – with which the joker's caricature is to be assessed and understood. This raises an important point: whereas contrast and distortion constitute the main principles for constructing secondary texts, *comparison* and *censure* appear to constitute the major principles for interpreting them. For what the joker intends is that the model he constructs of 'the Whiteman' will be judged and appraised in terms of models that members of his audience have of themselves as Apaches, and that this operation will reveal that, where versions of human guidedness are concerned, the Anglo-American version is not only different but also seriously defective.

In comparison to the behavior of Apaches, the joker invites his audience to see, the behavior of Whitemen is ineffectively guided and is therefore cause for amusement. But this same behavior, precisely because it is so liberally flawed with misdeeds and transgressions, can have damaging effects on the feelings of individuals. Consequently, it is also cause for disapproval and resentment.

That imitations of 'the Whiteman' are meant to convey this deprecatory message is clearly evident from a set of quasi-institutionalized expressions with which Apache butts are expected to respond at the conclusion of joking performances. Terse, aphoristic, and unequivocally critical – *indaa' dogoyą́ą́da* ('Whitemen are stupid') is a typical member of the set – these utterances function in several capacities at once. On the one hand, they signal to the joker that his actions have been appreciated in the spirit of play but that the joking frame should no longer be considered to apply. In effect, "the joke is over." On the other hand, and for our purposes more important, these expressions function as compact interpretations of the joker's model of 'the Whiteman', thus providing keys and guidelines ("ponies," if you will) that others may use to appraise his portrayal and draw from it appropriate conclusions of their own. As native readings of native texts, the responses of butts leave no doubt that joking imitations are intended as condemnations of what Apaches regard as conspicuous inadequacies in the social behavior of Anglo-Americans. In addition, these statements make explicit what some of the inadequacies are, and why, as a consequence of their maligning influence, dealing with Anglo-Americans can be a trying and painful experience.

The butts of joking performances customarily respond to them with one or more of the following expressions:

1. *indaa'* (Whitemen') *dogoyą́ą́da*. Literally, 'lacking in wisdom' or 'lacking in understanding', *dogoyą́ą́da* is com-

monly used in the senses of 'stupid', 'dumb', and 'foolish'. In addition, and especially when used in reference to Anglo-Americans, it connotes 'unthinking', 'unmindful', and 'oblivious'. *Interpretation and comment*: Whitemen lack self-awareness, a form of ignorance that blinds them to the effects their actions may have on other people.

2. *indaa*ˀ ('Whitemen') *doyaagoyą́ą́da.* Designating one aspect or manifestation of the 'lack of wisdom' labeled by *dogoyą́ą́da,* the form *doyaagoyą́ą́da* describes individuals whose behavior is observed to exhibit an absence of caution, attentiveness, and reserve. Thus, it is regularly employed in all of the following senses: 'careless', 'sloppy', 'clumsy', 'rash', 'impulsive', 'unconcerned', 'irresponsible', and 'inconsiderate'. *Interpretation and comment*: Whitemen lack circumspection and restraint, a shortcoming that leads them to behave with a kind of reckless self-centeredness that implies a basic disregard for the worth of other people.

3. *indaa*ˀ ('Whitemen') *dos*ˀ*aa bagochį́į́da.* Literally, 'quick to display anger', the expression *dos*ˀ*aa bagochį́į́da* is also employed in the senses of 'ill-tempered', 'easily offended', and 'unduly critical'. *Interpretation and comment*: Whitemen lack tolerance and equanimity, a deficiency that causes them to make harsh and precipitate judgments of other people.

4. *indaa*ˀ (Whitemen') *ˀadiłkąą.* A broad and flexible concept, *ˀadiłkąą* is applied to persons who suggest by whatever means – their demeanor, dress, the manner in which they live – that they may consider themselves superior to others. Thus, the term embraces a large number of related senses, including 'arrogant', 'conceited', 'proud', 'vain', 'boastful', 'supercilious', 'aloof', 'haughty', 'disdainful', 'contemptuous', and 'pretentious'. *Interpretation and comment:* Whitemen lack modesty and humility, a characteristic that causes them to adopt an attitude of imperiousness and condescension when dealing with other people.

5. *indaa*ˀ (Whitemen') *nant*ˀ*án* ˀ*agodil*ˀ*įį*. This expression, whose literal meaning is 'Whitemen act as if they were chiefs', is correctly interpreted in relation to the proposition that Anglo-Americans are *not* chiefs, and therefore have acquired neither the right nor the wisdom to give orders or unsolicited instructions to Western Apaches. Yet, as every Apache knows, they do so nonetheless. Consequently, *indaa*ˀ *nant*ˀ*án* ˀ*agodil*ˀ*įį* is understood in a sense roughly equivalent to 'Whitemen pretend to knowledge and status they do not possess'. *Interpretation and comment*: Whitemen lack an understanding of inadequacies inherent in their own forms of reasoning, a failing that leads them to

assume they know what is best for other people. In acting upon this assumption, they insult the intelligence of those they presume to advise.

6. *indaa*ˀ ('Whitemen') *donzhǫǫda*. Subtle, abstract, and richly polysemous, the term *nzhǫǫ* may be applied to any aspect of the Western Apache universe that is judged to be 'good', 'beautiful', or 'beneficial to man'. When used in reference to the conduct of human beings, *nzhǫǫ* implies predictability, dependability, cooperativeness, generosity, amiability, and courteousness. In reference to relations between human beings, it implies orderliness, stability, and harmony. Individuals whose actions fail to promote these conditions may be described by the expression *donzhǫǫda* (literally, 'lacking in goodness and beauty'), and thus, taken in a global sense, *indaa*ˀ *donzhǫǫda* may be glossed as follows: 'Whitemen conduct themselves in ways that are morally negligent, esthetically unpleasing, and detrimental to the establishment of productive social relations'. *Interpretation and comment*: Whitemen fail to appreciate the encompassing virtue of actions that affirm the dignity of other people, a shortcoming that manifests itself in behavior that accomplishes just the opposite and thus retards the development of confidence, respect, and goodwill.

These, then, are some of the cultural meanings communicated by joking imitations of Anglo-Americans. They are not the only meanings, and mine is not the only possible interpretation of them. But they are certainly among the meanings most frequently articulated by Western Apaches and, in their pointedness and lack of ambiguity, they provide a clear idea of the kinds of things that get said through the medium of joking performances. However one chooses to view these performances – as little rituals of reversal and inversion, of denial and rebellion, of affirmation and intensification – they are first and foremost expressive vehicles for constructing images of 'the Whiteman' and,

by means of these images, for ridiculing the behavior and
attitudes of Whitemen towards Apaches. And when they
are skillfully drawn – when the joker becomes intrigued
with the scene he is staging and temporarily loses himself
in the character he is portraying – the occasion is invested
with a dark and uncanny quality from which, if you happen
to be a Whiteman, you never quite recover. For you realize
instantly that Anglo-Americans, though rarely present in
Apache homes, are never really absent from them either.
'The Whiteman' can be brought to life at the drop of a joke,
and when he is thus epitomized at his inept worst – as a
loud-talking, overbearing, self-righteous, unswervingly presumptuous bumbler – you get to see him in a very special
way. He is indeed ridiculous, even absurd, and somehow,

always, oddly isolated and forlorn. But he is also a crude and insensitive boor.[27]

As portraits of 'the Whiteman' come alive, so do formulations of one of the most complex and powerful symbols in Western Apache culture. And if an outsider would understand a portion of what this symbol stands for and represents, then he or she, however skeptical, would be well

advised to attend carefully to the doings of jokers. For it is
a striking feature of Western Apache life that serious things
are always getting said in what appear to be unserious ways,
and Apache jokers, I have been implying all along, have
developed this practice into something of an art.[28] To be
sure, joking performances are "only" imitations, and they

tend to be fairly simple ones at that. But the relationship of these playful constructions to the more-pressing realities on which they are modeled is unfailingly deft and consistently credible; and thus joking imitations are altogether unique when viewed as cultural texts – as acted documents that give audible voice and visible substance to Apache conceptions of Anglo-Americans and the problems they face when they engage Anglo-Americans in social interaction.

Dramatizations of Western Apache experience, joking imitations are also Western Apache interpretations of it. And, like all successful dramatic forms, they entail a modification of experience in such a way that its significance can be more tellingly stated and more acutely perceived. By making of 'the Whiteman' an improbable buffoon, Apache jokers isolate and accentuate significant contrasts between their own cultural practices and those of Anglo-Americans. And by presenting the behavior of Anglo-Americans as something laughable and "wrong," by displaying with the help of butts how and why it violates the rights of others, they denounce these standards as morally deficient and unworthy of emulation.[29] In sum, joking performances make it emphatically clear that Whitemen and Western Apaches come to social encounters with conflicting ideas of what constitutes deferential comportment – ideas that are ultimately grounded in conflicting conceptions of what it means to be a person and the kinds of actions that can discredit a person's worth in public situations. On most occasions, perhaps, Apache jokers tell their fellows nothing about themselves and Anglo-Americans that they don't already know or suspect.[30] But they tell them about it in a manner that crisply reminds them of its enduring importance, and they urge them – without really coming out and saying so – never to forget it. Today, as in the past, 'the Whiteman' symbolizes an alien form of human guidedness. 'The Whiteman' is a symbol of what 'the Apache' is not.[31]

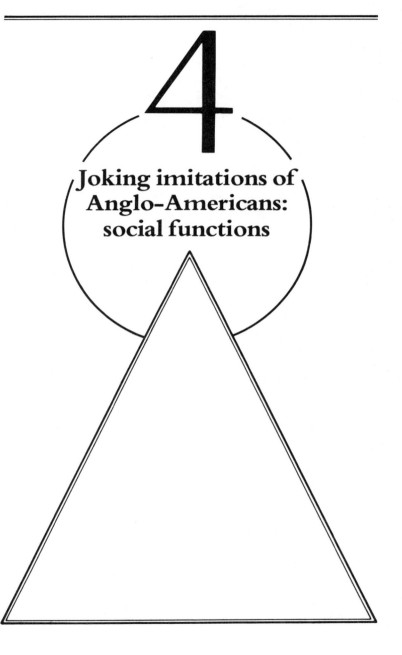

4

Joking imitations of Anglo-Americans: social functions

You must want to learn from your mother
You must listen to old men
not quite capable of becoming white men.

—David W. Martinez ("New Way, Old Way," *Voices from Wah'kon-tah*)

Having inquired into the interpretive functions of Western Apache joking imitations, we are now in a position to consider some of their pragmatic counterparts. What, in other words, of the social functions served by imitations of Anglo-Americans? What of the purposes these performances are used to accomplish in face-to-face encounters? In particular, what of the kinds of messages that joking imitations communicate about the persons who perform them and their relationship with individuals they cast in the role of butt? What, in short, of social meanings?

The social significance Western Apaches attach to joking is commonly discussed by them in terms of a traditional analogy that likens the development of solidarity in interpersonal relationships to the process by which 'deerhides' (*bįįh bi kágé*) are fashioned into pieces of fine 'buckskin' (*ʔiban*). Let us proceed, then, by describing this analogy and examining some of its implications. The basic premise is as follows: interpersonal relationships, like untanned hides, are initially 'stiff' (*ntłʔiz*) and therefore of little practical value; consequently, they must be gradually worked through successive stages of increasing pliability until, having become fully 'soft' (*diʔilé*), they become useful as well and can be counted on, given proper care and attention, to soften even further and become more useful still. Persons with 'stiff' relationships are typically those who have met only recently and, being anxious

67

not to offend each other, behave with cautious formality and studied respect. This is as it should be, Apaches point out, because 'stiff' relationships, like untanned hides, can be easily 'cracked' (*hisdla?*) and are frequently difficult to mend. At the other extreme, individuals who enjoy 'soft' relationships are those who have known each other for long periods of time, who have established sound bonds of mutual confidence and affection, and who, knowing this, feel free to take certain liberties which, in the context of less mature relationships, would be presumptuous and discourteous. This, too, is fitting, for although 'soft' relationships, like supple buckskins, are vulnerable to 'tears' (*yidzįįs*), they can usually be mended without excessive effort. In short, softness imparts resiliency and strength. And so it has been for quite some time.

One of my consultants, a man from Cibecue in his late fifties, said this:

A long time ago – they still made lots of buckskins then – when the women were making it, they talked to their children. "You see this deerhide?" they said. "Right now it's no good. Look at it – too stiff. I can't use it. That's why I'm going to make buckskin, so it will get soft. Maybe it's going to take a long time. I don't know. I'm going to start out real easy on it. If I don't go easy on it, maybe it's going to split itself." That's how those women would talk to their children. "Same way it is with people around here," they said. "With them, it's like this deerhide – too stiff. Don't count on these people right away, even your own young relatives. Maybe they won't want to help you. So you got to work on them like I'm working on this dried-up deerhide. Then it's going to get soft and strong between you. Go easy when you start out. Don't talk smart. Don't ask for any-

thing. Just talk good. That's the right way. Then,
after a while you can start to fool around. Then it
don't matter too much. It's like pulling on some
buckskin – you do that and you just make it softer."
That's how those old women used to talk. Not many
make buckskins now, but it don't matter. What they
said was good, so we keep on saying it.

Expanding on their analogy, Apaches assert that joking is
one means for 'stretching' (*náádi'tso'*) social relationships,
a playful device for testing and affirming solidarity by
ostensibly denying it. However, they are quick to observe
that for this very reason – that jokes are not what they
seem, that they are 'bad words' (*nchǫǫ' yałti'*) in humorous
disguise – joking can also accomplish the opposite effect; it
can 'tear' relationships as well. For however amusing a joke
may be, it is always amusing at someone's expense; and
therefore, unless jokers are careful to keep their bogus
slurs and criticisms within properly playful limits, their
actions may be interpreted as veiled expressions of genuine
hostility. In short, there is always a possibility that persons
who appear to be joking may not be joking at all, and this
is why, as mentioned earlier, Apaches claim that joking can
be 'dangerous' (*benagodzig'*).[32]

Another consultant from Cibecue commented on this
point in greater detail:

Some people hide behind their joking. Some talk bad
right to your face and try to get away with it. Sometimes, like when they drink too much, you just don't
know. You just can't tell for sure. Maybe they just
pretend they joking. That's when some people get
mad. "Come out or don't say nothing to me!" That's
why you just got to go easy on it. You don't go easy
and somebody's going to get mad. That's danger,
right there.

At this point, it might appear as if the paradox inherent in joking behavior causes the buckskin analogy to break down. After all, how is it that an activity that functions to affirm solidarity can also function to weaken it? Apaches maintain that the answer is simple and noncontradictory. Just as the worker of deerhides should not attempt to hasten the tanning process by taking shortcuts or leaving out essential steps, so should the parties to freshly founded social relationships allow ample time to pass before they start to joke. For it is perfectly evident, Apaches contend, that 'stiff' relationships are less amenable to 'stretching' than those that have been partially 'softened', and therefore it follows necessarily that mock insults are more apt to produce 'tears' in the former than in the latter. In other words, joking is more likely to arouse suspicion and resentment during the formative stages of a relationship than it is later on when solidarity has been firmly established. And since Apaches hold that true solidarity does not develop rapidly, it stands to reason that joking is best postponed until less precipitous means of testing it have been tried and proved effective. Men, like buckskins, cannot be rushed into softness.

Said one of my consultants:

> You know somebody real good – it's soft like buckskin between you – he won't think about it when you joke. You joke him, it's just going to bounce off like nothing. He's going to laugh, maybe joke you back. He knows you just saying it. With some others – you don't know them too good, don't see them long time, live some other place, like that – maybe they don't want it. Maybe they get mad, think you hiding. With them, you got to wait. After that, you can try some joking. Go easy on it. After that, they not going to think about it. It's just going to bounce off like nothing. With some, you got to wait a long time.

Just as social relationships are seen by Western Apaches to vary in degrees of softness, so, too, different forms of joking are understood to vary in their capacity to engender antagonism and ill will. In other words, certain kinds of jokes are considered intrinsically more insulting, and therefore more obviously 'dangerous', than others. Among the most 'dangerous' of all are those of the *banagozdi²* variety in which the joker takes on the indentity of someone who indicates by his disrespectful treatment of the butt that he thinks of himself as being better – or, as Apaches prefer to say, 'higher' (*k²ago*) – than other people. For while Apaches acknowledge that they distinguish openly among themselves according to differences in economic, political, and religious status, they are adamant in their insistence that none of these differences is of sufficient importance to warrant or justify smug displays of personal superiority. Outside the world of joking such displays occur infrequently. But when they do, word spreads quickly and those at fault are criticized with a vociferous intensity that can be truly alarming. "People who rise above others should not look down," Apaches warn. "People who know what's right treat everyone the same."

The characters portrayed in joking imitations of Anglo-Americans are cited by Apaches as prime examples of people who 'look down' (*des²ąą des²įį*) on others, and thus it is not surprising that the butts of joking performances react to them with less than total enthusiasm. For even in jest, Apaches say, there is always something unpleasant about subordinating oneself to a 'Whiteman'.[33] What is unpleasant, of course, is the close relation between the secondary texts constructed by jokers and the primary texts on which they have been modeled. Too often, in real encounters with real Anglo-Americans, the butts of jokes have been treated with insolence and disdain. Too often, they have been prematurely hailed as "friends," or asked how they feel, or rudely stared at, or summarily "bossed around," or invasively slapped on the back. Too often, Anglo-Americans have made Apaches "feel small," and being reminded of this, even in fun, is never entirely funny.

Sometimes, and especially when heavy drinking is involved, this kind of joking may stir a butt to anger. Unwittingly or not, the joker slips up. His caricature of 'the Whiteman' is too convincing or not quite convincing enough. His joke may go on for what seems too long a time, or he may give the impression that he is enjoying himself just a bit too much. And suddenly, for whatever reason, doubt intrudes upon the fragile world of play and the butt suspects that the joker may be "hiding" behind his joke. Instantly, the fiction the joker has established starts to crumble and ritual patina that has previously framed his actions begins to dissolve. His joke, which is a joke no longer, is taken as a personal affront, an authentic insult, a camouflaged expression of scorn. A relationship has been 'stretched' too far – and it 'tears'.

Several years ago, on the Fort Apache Reservation, a man was beaten up, and later on, when I was talking with his assailant, the latter recalled that he had become infuriated when he was "joked like a Whiteman."

> I don't remember too good because I was drinking. We were sitting around drinking beer. Pretty soon, that man started in on joking us, just kind of easy. Nobody think about it. Then he started in on me. I don't know him too good so I wonder what he's doing. Pretty soon, he went into English and act like he was some trader or something. "Pay you bill, no more credit." Like that. He keep on saying it. He's going to stop pretty quick, I think, so I don't say nothing. "Pay your bill." Same way, he keep on saying it. "Stop," I told him. Same way, he keep on going. Then I

just went crazy or something, too much beer, so
I jumped on him.

If joking, as A. R. Radcliffe-Brown suggested, is characterized in all societies by exhibitions of "privileged licence"
and "permitted disrespect," it is only because those who
engage in such exhibitions are everywhere under strong
obligations not to abuse their privileges or to exceed the
limits of what is locally defined as permissibly disrespectful.
For when these obligations are ignored – when, as we
sometimes say, jokers "press too hard" or "go too far" –
those whose expectations have been violated may exercise
their right to express displeasure and, in extreme cases,
may retaliate in ways that precipitate explosive incidents
like the one described above. Among the Western Apache,
such incidents are very rare. Most of the time, Apache
jokers go about their business in a distinctly conservative
manner, their forays into the world of play causing little,
if any, visible social disturbance. But the fact remains
that the line between mock insults and real ones can become precariously thin, and nowhere, Apaches claim, is
this more likely to happen than in joking imitations of
Anglo-Americans. For such is the antipathy of Apaches to
being 'looked down' upon that even the mildest displays
of arrogance and self-importance may trigger strong reactions. And since the 'Whitemen' who appear in jokes are
nothing if not arrogant and self-important, the persons
who portray them inevitably tread on sensitive ground.

Thus, imitations of Anglo-Americans entail a degree
of risk that only persons with fully softened relationships
are normally prepared to take. It is for this reason, Apaches
explain, that joking imitations tend to occur infrequently.
And it is also for this reason that most joking encounters
involve individuals who have been acquainted since child-
hood – older men, usually members of the same community,

who have grown up together, worked together, sung together, drunk together, and through it all, thick and thin, have come to share a degree of fondness and concern for one another that only the most serious of social offenses could threaten or destroy. These men have 'stretched' their relationships about as far as relationships can be 'stretched', and thus the possibility is small that untoward jokes – even jokes that backfire badly – will result in serious 'tears'. Consequently, such individuals are able to joke 'dangerously' with an enviable measure of impunity, and they regard it, especially before a large audience, as a way of 'boasting' (*ʔadiɬkąąyo yaɬtiʔ*) about the closeness of their ties.

In this connection, Apaches draw a final implication from the buckskin analogy. To wit: persons who have cultivated 'soft' relationships, like those who have worked hard to produce fine buckskins, take pride in their accomplishments and enjoy calling attention to them. In both cases, however, anything that resembles straightforward bragging is criticized. An alternative for owners of buckskins is to treat their prized possessions with apparent disregard, tugging on them roughly and complaining to all within earshot that they remain stubbornly stiff. Similarly, individuals with 'soft' relationships may display this achievement by subjecting each other to strong forms of feigned verbal abuse, including, most conspicuously, the several varieties of *banagozdiʔ*. 'Boasting' it may be. But like so many other things Apache, it is 'boasting' of an oblique and circuitous kind, which, betraying not the slightest trace of complacency or self-satisfaction, appears on the surface to be something else entirely. Irony abounds and Apaches appreciate it well.

Said a man from Cibecue, himself an inveterate joker:

> Us old men get to joking like that – it's sure funny to us. Some do it more than others. Some really like it.

They do everything – act like Whiteman, everything.
They boss you around, act like you nothing, right in
front lots of people. Only we don't get mad. They just
boasting, that's all. Just saying it, that's all. We been
going around long time together, so we done it before.
That's why people like to watch us. What we doing
sure looks bad. We don't mean it. It's good. Us men
call each other anything. It don't matter. We been
going around long time together. It's good. We don't
see no danger.

There are many things one can get called in Western
Apache culture, and there are numerous ways to joke
'dangerously'. But none is potentially more hazardous
(and therefore, it may be added, more certain to delight
Apache audiences) than that which requires butts to sub-
mit to demeaning treatment at the hands of bogus 'Whitemen'. Only men whose relationships have become very
'soft' feel privileged to engage in this kind of play, for it
is understood to proceed from a mutual affection so
strongly felt and fundamentally secure that it can safely
risk expression in a manner that transforms its object from
the respected companion he is into a figure deserving of
no respect at all. But, of course, the transformation is
only an illusion. Apache jokers are not expected to intend
what their actions appear to mean. Rather, they are assumed to intend just the reverse. Accordingly, the scenes
jokers stage are interpreted as emphatic illustrations of
what their relationship with the butt is not, and the characters they portray – those fatuous, self-serving, unshakably
superior 'Whitemen' – are construed as sharp-edged depic-
tions of individuals whose values and attitudes differ radically
from their own. In this way, as one of my consultants observed, "People who joke like Whitemen turn everything
around." Herein lies the gist of the social meanings communicated by joking imitations of Anglo-Americans. A

relationship in which goodwill is abundantly present is represented as one in which it is conspicuously absent. And an individual who normally refrains from 'looking down' on other people portrays himself as one who 'looks down' with no compunctions at all. Everything is turned around.

But such goings on are commonplace in what Barbara Babcock (1978) has aptly termed the "reversible world" of play. The products of solidarity and commitment, joking imitations are inverted celebrations of them as well. These performances are little morality plays in which Western Apaches affirm their conceptions of what is "right" and proper by dramatizing their conceptions of what is "wrong" and inappropriate. Concomitantly, they affirm their sentiments for one another, and nothing, they would claim, is more important. But jokers must be careful. For however paradoxical it may be, men, like buckskins, may suffer damage from too much playful abuse. And as an Apache from Cibecue remarked, "Whitemen can make trouble even when they're not around."[34]

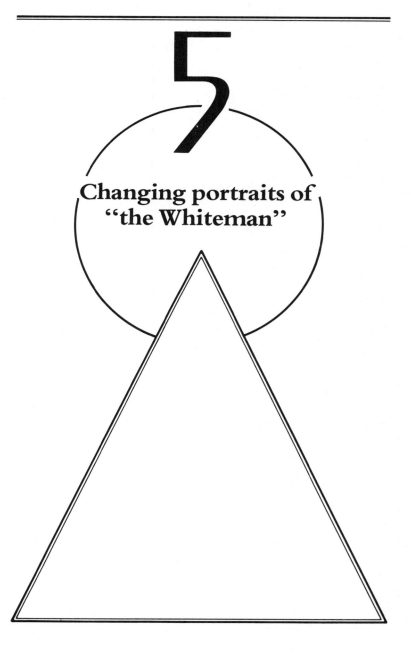

5

Changing portraits of "the Whiteman"

> When a people can laugh at themselves and others
> and hold all aspects of life together without letting
> anybody drive them to extremes, then it seems to
> me that people can survive.
>
> —Vine Deloria, Jr. (*Custer Died for Your Sins: An Indian Manifesto*)

Like everything else sociocultural, systems of morality and the symbols in which they find expression are subject to modification and change. Here, too, Western Apache joking performances are instructive. I began investigating imitations of Anglo-Americans in the summer of 1965, and although I did not pursue the project with the diligence I now wish I had, the early materials suggest some interesting things. It is clear, for example, that the characters portrayed in jokes are almost always role-specific, and that the fabricated encounters in which these characters appear are highly sensitive to current events. Like political cartoonists and calypso singers, Apache jokers make a point of keeping up with the times.

In 1966 and 1967, Apaches at Cibecue portrayed 'the Whiteman' as hippie – mumbling, awkwardly effeminate, and, as one of my consultants put it, "rich but pretending poor." In 1970, VISTA volunteers descended on the community, and before long they were also providing materials for secondary texts. 'The Whiteman' as VISTA worker was gushingly altruistic, hopelessly incompetent at simple manual tasks, and, for some reason I was never able to pin down, invariably out of breath. And then there was a team of physicians from a medical center at an eastern university who came to Cibecue to stamp out diarrhea in infants, and also – and here I quote from a hand-lettered sign that appeared at the time in trading posts – to "educate mothers in the proper techniques of breast feeding." In the understated manner that Western Apaches typically assume when speaking to Anglo-Americans, it was pointed out that pursuit of the latter objective was unnecessary. But the doctors persisted, and shortly thereafter, having been given the less-than-flattering title of 'those who play with babies' shit' (*me ? bi chą yenagołdéhé*), they, too, became the subject of joking imitations.[35] And so have schoolteachers, nurses, missionaries, trading-post owners, social workers, sawmill foremen, tourists, stockmen, construction bosses, and, all too probably, a certain ethnographer from the University of Arizona.

This suggests that it would be not quite right to adopt the view held by large numbers of American sociologists and say that Western Apache jokers are simply "acting out" a set of prefigured ethnic stereotypes. Such a view is misleading because it obscures the inventive and interpretive components that figure so prominently in joking performances; it is too static and mechanical. What impresses me, comparing last year's jokes with those of years before, is that Apache portraits of 'the Whiteman' are unfailingly contemporary and consistently experimental. In other words, the symbol is continuously acquiring fresh significations, while older ones, no longer considered apt or fully up-to-date, are permitted to slough off and fade away. Thus, what we catch glimpses of is an ongoing process of change in which conceptions of 'the Whiteman' – and, it seems reasonable to suppose, conceptions of 'the Apache' as well – are being assessed and reassessed, formulated and reformulated, modified and modified again. It follows necessarily that Western Apache jokers are properly regarded as more than mere purveyors of preexisting cultural forms. They are creators of culture as well, and serve in this capacity as active agents of cultural change.

If attending to joking imitations of Anglo-Americans can increase our understanding of aspects of Western Apache culture, it can also increase our understanding of aspects of our own. For whether we like it or not, the Apache, like other groups of Indians living throughout the United States, regard Anglo-Americans as a problem, and some of the reasons why may not be readily apparent. To be sure, Whitemen have stolen land, violated treaties, and on numerous other fronts treated Indians with a brutal lack of awareness and concern. But these are not the messages communicated by Western Apache jokers. Their sights are trained on something more basic, and that is making sense of how Anglo-Americans conduct themselves in the presence of Indian people. Here, too, Whitemen are frequently found guilty of incompetence and gross neglect.

And this, finally, is what the cultural meanings of Apache joking performances are all about. Commentaries in carica-ture about perceived deficiencies in an alien form of human guidedness, imitations of Anglo-Americans are also state-ments about what can happen to dignity and self-respect when two systems of sharply discrepant cultural norms collide in social encounters. In the long run, the damage done by such collisions may be just as injurious as mis-handled disputes over water rights, land claims, and the sovereignty of native courts. And as far as the private feelings of individuals are concerned, I fear the damage may be worse. But enough. A joke, after all, is a joke. And one must be careful not to stretch a relationship too far. Accordingly, I should like to conclude, just as a Western Apache joker might, with a reminder that the whole thing has been in fun – but then, paradoxically, not really. "Hello, my friend, how you doing?"

Appendix

The purpose of this Appendix is to illustrate the range of characters portrayed in Western Apache joking imitations of Anglo-Americans, and to provide supplementary information about the kinds of cultural contrasts these performances serve to highlight and interpret. Besides the four imitations described in the body of the essay, I witnessed eight others. Accounts of seven of these are presented below, together with reports of seven additional performances (selected from among a total of twenty-nine that were witnessed by Apache consultants. I cannot claim that my accounts are entirely faithful or fully complete. Western Apache jokers ply their trade on the spur of the moment, and, in most cases, conclude their imitations less than a minute after beginning them. Usually, it is possible to take note of most that has happened – but never all of it.

1. A 'physician' (*izee? nant?án*).
   Setting: A ramada at an Apache camp in Cibecue.
   Participants: A (male, age 29); B, A's brother-in-law (age 33); and KHB.
   Scene: A is sitting in the shade of the ramada, leafing idly through the pages of a comic book. B, who has recently injured his hand in a fall from a horse, enters the ramada and sits down. He examines his hand, which is wrapped in a bandage that has become soiled and dirty.

A: *gostoodʾ né?* ('It's hot, isn't it'?)

B: *ʾaa. gostoodʾ.* ('Yes. It's hot'.)

A: *nigan ndiih né?* ('Does your hand hurt'?)

B: *ʾaa.* ('Yes'.)

A: Why you go let that cloth get dirty? No good! You sit right there, my friend. I take care of you. I know everything! What happen? You been drinking too much?

B: *ʾą́ą́ɬ* ('That's enough'.)

A: [Ignoring B's request to stop joking] Maybe you been fighting – that's why you get all dirty. Maybe you got family problem. Maybe your wife get after you. Come here. I fix everything.
[A rises, walks to where B is seated, and pretends to bandage the latter's hand with the comic book.]

B: *ʾą́ą́ɬ. ʾą́ą́ɬ. indaaʾ ʾadiɬkąą* ('Enough. Enough. Whitemen are arrogant'.)

If Anglo-Americans are too inquisitive by Western Apache standards (see no. 2, Sect. 3), they are also overly accusatory. Physicians are taken to epitomize this tendency, as shown in this performance by queries and comments such as *You been drinking too much?* and *Maybe you been fighting*. Questions and statements of this kind also signify a willingness to jump to conclusions on the basis of insufficient evidence (e.g., *Maybe you got family problem*), a predilection that is seen to result from the conviction of physicians that they possess superior powers of intelligence (e.g., *I know everything!*).

2. A 'schoolteacher' (*bik ʾeho dagoɬtááge*).

Setting: A roundup camp approximately six miles from the community of Cibecue.

Participants: Seven male Apaches, including C (age 46) and D (age 40), and KHB.

Scene: It is just after lunch and the men, who have worked hard since dawn, are resting. C has lain down on his bedroll and has closed his eyes. D, seated nearby, is inspecting a lasso. Presently, D places the rope aside and kicks C gently on the boot.

D: Get up! Get up, you sleepyhead! Cheer up, lazy boy, the sun is red!
   [B opens his eyes and stares, smiling, at the sky above him.]

D: Get up and brush your teeth. I want you to get clean clothes. Comb you dirty hair! Wash you hands! How come you so lazy, dirty all the time. You hear me? Go wash you hands!

B: [Turning to lie on his side and closing his eyes again] *hiyaa. hiyaa. indaaˀ dogoyą́ą́da.* (I'm tired. I'm tired. Whitemen are stupid'.)

In the opinion of many Apaches, Anglo-Americans exhibit excessive concern with matters pertaining to personal hygiene. This is harmless enough. What is resented (and what this joking performance is intended to condemn) is that schoolteachers, who have earned the reputation of being obsessed with cleanliness, sometimes comment critically on the appearance of their pupils, apparently believing that by shaming them in public they will be inspired to develop tidier habits. Rarely, I am told, is this tactic successful; and occasionally, as the incident described in the following passage makes clear, it can produce just the opposite of its intended effect.

Two years back, my boy went to school. He's in fourth grade then. It's rain hard that morning, and he's got long way to walk, so he's real muddy when he gets there. Right away, the teacher gets after him, so he's feeling bad 'cause he's all dirty. After that, at lunchtime, he go outside and put mud all in his hair and shirt. Then he's go back in. All them children laugh 'cause they know why he done it. That teacher sure get after him again, but now he don't mind it.

3. A 'trader' (*diyage yasidááhi*).
Setting: A drinking party on the porch of an Apache home at Cibecue.
Participants: Fourteen adult Apaches, including E (male, age 35) and F, E's female matrilateral cross-cousin (age 42); eight children; and KHB.
Scene: E is speaking with several of the men present when F, who has been in the house, comes outside to join the party. She is freshly dressed and is wearing two silver-and-turquoise bracelets on her wrist.

E: Look, my friends, somebody just come in over here! Hello, F. Hello, hello, hello. You sure looking good dress up today, F. Pretty good, all right. Pretty good bracelet you wearing today. Where you get them? [F, who is smiling, places her hand over the jewelry on her arm.]

E: I sure like them bracelet, look like old-timer. Why you want to hide them? Lemme see, lemme see. Yep, sure it's old-timer. Good stone, good blue stone. I never see them before, F, where you get them? Maybe you want some new shoes.

F: *dohwhaada!* ('Nothing for me'!)

It is a tacit understanding shared by all Western Apaches that to openly admire another person's possessions is to express a wish to own them. And to lavish praise upon an object, as E's 'trader' does in this performance, is equivalent to requesting it as a gift or to making an offer to buy it. Where items of personal adornment are concerned, effusive appreciation is especially inappropriate because it sets up a situation in which the owner must either part with valued belongings or, by refusing, expose himself as one who is less than fully generous, although generosity is a value to which

Apaches attach great importance. Most Anglo-Americans are not aware of the predicament in which Apaches find themselves, but traders and storekeepers, many of whom have lived among the people for years, will sometimes try to exploit it in order to secure items that can later by sold at a handsome profit. Apaches see through this underhanded strategy and except when extremely hardpressed for cash have none of it.

4. A 'tourist' (*tooris*).

Setting: A drinking party on the bank of Cibecue Creek.
Participants: Six adult Apaches, including G (male, age 27) and H (male, age 36); two children; and KHB.
Scene: It is early evening and a gentle breeze is blowing. G, who has left the group to urinate, returns at the same time that H, who is ready to go home, stands up to leave

H: *nadistsaa.* ('I'm going home'.)

G: Don't go away yet, my Indian friend. You going to miss sunset. Sure pretty good. You see it? Look at sun, look at clouds, look at stars. You see it? Just like postcard. You see it? Good wind. Nice and cool. You feel it? You sure lucky live over here. Sure beautiful country. You lucky Indian, my friend. I sorry you got to go.

[Everyone present laughs heartily, including H.]

H: *indaaʔ doyaagoyą́ą́da.* ('Whitemen lack restraint'.)

According to Western Apaches, it is a peculiar habit of Anglo-Americans that they discourse at length on the patently obvious (see no. 9, Sect. 3), an inclination that finds one of its purest expressions in the excited gushings of tourists and other visitors to the Fort Apache Reservation. Unfortunately, when these spasms of enthusiasm are directed at Apaches, they may take offense, for what is implied, they claim, is that they have been judged insensitive to the beauty of their own homeland (e.g., *Look at sun, look at clouds, look at stars*) and need to be *told* that it is a region of unsurpassing natural splendor. Gratuitous instruction of this kind is totally uncalled for, and Apaches regard it as yet another form of Anglo-American condescension.

5. A 'sawmill foreman' (*saamil nant ʔán*).
   Setting: A drinking party on the bank of Cibecue Creek.
   Participants: Four adult Apaches, all of them brothers, including I (age 38) and J (age 40–45); and KHB.
   Scene: It is around ten o'clock on a cool September night and the men are seated around a small fire. I, who has left the group to collect some more wood, stumbles as he returns and the sticks he is carrying fall to the ground.
   J: [Responding instantly] Goddamn, I, how come you get drunk? How come you drink too much? You shit worker around here, always drinking too much. I give you lots of warning, all the time same way. Shit! How come you don't care nothing for your family? You fired! Get away from here. I don't want you at this sawmill no more!
   I: [Smiling as he gathers up the firewood] *nadistsaa. nadistsaa.* ('I'm going home. I'm going home'.)
       [I, still smiling, sits down, and after a brief period of silence, conversation switches to another topic.]

Apaches living at Cibecue report that when they are working for Anglo-Americans and something goes wrong on the job, their employers frequently react by attributing the trouble to the actions of a "drunk Indian." On some occasions, such accusations are justified; most times, they are not. Nevertheless, my consultants insist, the idea persists among Whitemen that Apaches are fundamentally irresponsible (e.g., *How come you don't care nothing for your family?*), and that they will seek intoxication whenever the opportunity presents itself. This is simply untrue. More serious still, Anglo-Americans in positions of authority will sometimes use drunkenness as a fabricated excuse to fire Apaches to whom they have taken a personal dislike. This is unforgivable.

6. A VISTA volunteer (no Western Apache term).
   Setting: An Apache camp in Cibecue.
   Participants: K (male, age 37); L, K's wife (age 28); L's two sisters (ages 29 and 41); five children; and KHB.
   Scene: It is a hot afternoon in August and the three women are seated together in the shade of a large tree. K, who is attempting to repair a broken fuel pump on his pickup truck, stands a few yards away. Suddenly, he gives a soft cry of disgust and holds up his finger, which has suffered a superficial cut.

   L: *ndiih né?* ('Is it painful'?)
   K: *dah* ('No'.)
      [K reaches into his pocket, withdraws a handkerchief, and wraps it around his injured finger. Then, feigning a look of alarm, he turns and addresses his wife.]
   K: Oh, damn, look what I done it! I come over here, try to fix you car. That car hurt me, cut my hand. Bad car! Why it do that to me! No good, you damn car!
      [At this point, K delivers a kick to the vehicle's front tire.]
   K: I trying to fix you! Damn car! You better watch out! You going to get it one of these days!
      [K is finished. The three women break into loud laughter.]

This joking performance is intended to ridicule an aspect of Anglo-American behavior that Apaches find mysterious and extremely odd: Whitemen get angry at machines and berate them when they break down. There is nothing more to the joke than this, but this is enough to make it hilarious.

7. A BIA bureaucrat (no Western Apache term).
   Setting: A drinking party in an Apache home at Cibecue.
   Participants: Nine adult Apaches, including M (male, age 47) and N, M's brother-in-law (age 35); at least five children; and KHB.
   Scene: M, who is standing unobtrusively in a corner, takes a piece of paper from his shirt pocket and begins to read it. N observes this and calls out to M in a loud voice.

   N: You got trouble reading, my friend? Lemme see. I going to help you.
      [N walks to where M is standing and takes the paper from him. He holds it out before him and pretends to study it carefully. Then he turns and addresses M.]

   N: This your form one hundred. No, maybe one hundred forty-three. Maybe thirty-six. I just don't know. You got to make application for seventy-two, seventy-three, seventy-four. You get it tomorrow, my friend, deadline pretty quick. Hurry up!
      [M smiles and shakes his head in amused resignation. N then launches into nonsense.]

   N: No occupation steps . . . benefits line right here . . . qualification experience . . . work training function. See my friend, like that! Just you read instructions. Real easy. Now you know it, see? I help you out.
      [M reaches for the paper N is holding and takes it back.]

   M: ʾąąl. indaaʾ dogoyą́ą́da. ('Enough. Whitemen are stupid'.)

Anglo-Americans who work for the Bureau of Indian Affairs on the Fort Apache Reservation are sometimes called upon to assist Apaches when they fill out applications for jobs, welfare benefits, and other governmental services. However, some of these employees fail to recognize that most Apaches are totally unfamiliar with the language such documents contain – *indaaʔ bi yatiʔ nchaahi* ('Whiteman's big words') – and that many of the people have difficulty reading them. Consequently, as this joking performance is meant to show, the assistance given by Anglo-Americans may be of no use at all. And when it is delivered in the flippant and imperious manner of the character portrayed by N, Apaches become resentful. One of my consultants commented on the problem as follows:

> Some of them Whitemen over at Whiteriver [site of BIA headquarters] just use big words to us. We don't know what they saying. It don't mean nothing to us. So we have trouble making out them papers. Some people just give up on it. Lots of these people can't read good, write good. Some of them Whitemen say they going to help you out, but all they know is big words so they can't do nothing. Some act like you real dumb. We get mad when they do that.

Accounts of Joking Imitations by Western Apaches

The following descriptions of joking performances are valuable in two respects. First, they present useful information about the performances themselves. Second, they contain brief interpretations by the Apaches who witnessed and reported them. Most of these interpretations are concise, clear, and fully to the point, thus requiring little or nothing in the way of supporting commentary.

1. A 'physician' (*izeeʔ nantʔán*). Old A (male, age 55), he done like that one time. He's drinking at B's place, lots of people over there. So he's feeling good and starts in on C (male, age 50–55). He's act like he's some doctor 'cause he's ask him how much he do it with his wife. He's saying, "I got to put it on your record. Got to put it on your record." Like that. Sure crazy. Some of them doctors

try to ask you anything, even like that. They always want
to write it down. We don't like it, so we don't say nothing.
It's no good.

2. A 'missionary' (*ïïnashood˘*). D (male, age 49) joke
like that one time two years ago. He's start in on E (male,
age 42). E's marry with D's sister long time ago, got five
children with her. So D acts like some missionary, starts
cussing E out. "How come you still living in sin, my brother?
You been with my sister long time. How come you still got
no paper [i.e., marriage license]? You no good Christian,
my brother, no good Christian." He goes on like that. Sure
pretty funny. We all laughing at him. D cuss his brother-in-
law 'cause he got no paper! Whiteman crazy.

3. A 'nurse' (*izee˘ isdzán*). One time, down below at X's
place, H (male, age 48–50) joke like that on I (male, age 37).
I's real thin, been like that since he's little boy, thin and
tall. So there's lots of people down there, and H starts
talking like some nurse. He's talk like I's too fat. "You
eat too much bad Indian food, make you too fat. Too
much pop, too much beans, too much bread. How come
you don't care how you looking? No exercise, too much
drink, just lie around all the time. Pretty soon you going
to get trouble – high blood pressure, sugar diabetes."

This performance catches up several themes previously
discussed. See especially numbers 8 and 9, Sect. 3 of the
text, and number 5, in the first section of this Appendix.

4. A 'hippie' (*indaa˘ diwóózhe*; 'hairy Whiteman').
I'm walking home that time, not too late. J's calling me
from his place, "Come over here. Come over here and drink
some beer." So I walk over there, sit down, start drinking.
Pretty soon, others come over there, start drinking. J
(age 36), he's feeling good 'cause pretty soon he starts
in joking me (male, age 47) like some Whiteman. I know
he's just joking. He's done like that before, lots of times.
This time, he's act like some hippie. He's put a mop on

his head – long hair. Then he's walk around me where I'm sitting, look me over, stare at me, like that. He don't say nothing. Then he's start in talking to me. "You native American, man, first citizen. Wow. Wow." He just keep saying it, "Wow." Then he's ask me for money. "Gimme one dollar, fifty cents, one dime. You my brother, you my brother." Sure all them people really laughing at J's doing to me. Hippie says he's my brother! He say that 'cause he just want money, that's all. Some Whitemen still think us Indians is dumb.

5. A 'policeman' (*ʔaasatíni*). That man, L (age 62), he's get old now. He's real funny when he's joking. Last time I seen him do it, he's down at his place. His wife's cooking outside. He's been drinking some home brew, so I think maybe he's going to start in joking. He don't do nothing, just talking. Then, his grandson (age 6) start pulling his little wagon around – back and forth, back and forth. L don't do nothing, just watch that little boy. Then, after a while, he stand up and go into English, act like some police. "Stop! Stop!" He's talking loud. "You driving too fast. Maybe you drunk. Maybe you got some woman with you, not your wife!" So he's arrest his grandson, like that. That little boy's get scared, I guess. He start to cry. Everybody's sure laughing . . . Sometimes, even you doing nothing, those police haul you over, say bad things, want to know what you been doing. Just 'cause you Indian they look down on you like that.

6. A 'dancer' (*gotaałe*). One time, it's spring, lots of people were planting corn. I was with my brother. We were planting my mother's field for her. Later, in the afternoon, we walked back to her place. Lots of people went together. When we got there, we started having a good time – singing, dancing, everybody's feeling good. We were singing Apache songs for corn, make it grow up good. Then, after a while, somebody's turn on the radio in my mother's house – real

loud, rock and roll. Right away, O (male, age 42) start dancing like some Whiteman. It looks like he's crazy! He's start jumping around, wave his arms, start shouting. "Hang it out! Hang it out!" He's shouting it real loud. He's push his ass in and out, looks like he's trying to screw. It's like he's crazy. Some ladies there don't want to look at it, get up, walk away. Everybody's really laughing. It looks so *bad*! Then, he goes over to where P (male, age 30) is sitting next to his wife. "Hey, my friend, you want to dance with me?" he says to P. "I been thinking a lot about you. These people sure gonna like it, you dance with me." P don't like it, so he's talk Apache, says, "Go away. Go away. Get away from me, you crazy Whiteman." Then he's start laughing.

7. (A non-role-specific joking performance.) Some White-men sure think they big shots, so they dress up real good all the time, wear fancy clothes, cost lots of money. So last year, one time, F (male, age 47), he's been working on irrigation ditch. He's wearing old shirt, old hat, got lots of mud on his pants. Dirty all over. So he's stop on his way home at G's place, drink some beer. Pretty soon, G (male, age 42) start in joking like that, imitate some Whiteman. He's go into English, talking to F. "You sure got good shirt, my friend, real good hat, good pants. How much you pay for them? Let me buy them from you." He's talk like that. He's act like G's all dressed up, only he's real dirty! Apaches don't talk how someone's look to his face. Some people around here still pretty poor, got no money for good clothes. So we don't say nothing about that, don't notice how they look. It's different with Whitemen.

Notes

Notes to Foreword

1. *Gifted* is the word my wife and I know for this, from friends at Warm Springs, Oregon. It fills a lexical gap in English (Basso, 1976) in providing a unitary transitive verb to name the active step in a cycle of exchange.
2. Sapir's major article, still stimulating, is "Abnormal Types of Speech among the Nootka" (1915). He noted devices of characterization that reflect neighboring peoples also in Takelma; see Hymes (1979). The only sequel at the time was Frachtenberg (1917).
3. These remarks agree with Lévi-Strauss in finding abstract analysis in myths, but differ in imputing awareness of intention, focused on interpersonal relations and reflecting personal historical situations, analogous to the awareness and focus of the Apache portraits of 'whiteman'. This is not to deny that his principle of transformation in myth is a fundamental discovery.

Notes to text

1. English terms and phrases enclosed in single quotation marks are *glosses*, devices that facilitate discussion of Western Apache conceptions without using the Apache linguistic forms (or morpheme-by-morpheme translations) that represent them. Thus, the terms 'Whiteman' and 'Whitemen', both of which are represented by

indaaʔ, are employed to label Apache conceptions of Anglo-Americans and/or the characters that give expression to these conceptions in joking performances. Without quotation marks, the terms designate Anglo-Americans themselves.

2. Schutz used this phrase in several papers dealing with subjective meaning, cross-cultural interpretation, and what he called the "problem of social reality." See, for example, Schutz, 1944, 1953, and 1954.

3. I use the term *symbol* in the broad and flexible sense described by David Schneider (1968) and Clifford Geertz (1973a, 1976). See Geertz (1966) for a clear discussion of symbols as models and the utility of distinguishing between their "of" and "for" components. In a recent statement, Schneider (1976) draws an analogous distinction that helps to clarify the normative (i.e., "for") aspects of symbolic constructions.

4. This is particularly clear in recent literary works by American Indians as well as in their social criticism. See, for example, Momaday (1969), Ortiz (1974), Silko (1977), Walsh (1974), and Welch (1974). A useful ethnographic statement is found in Braroe (1975).

5. The phrase "cultural portraits of ourselves" appears in notes I took as a student in Social Sciences 5 (Introduction to the Social Sciences), a course given for undergraduates by Clyde Kluckhohn and Henry A. Murray at Harvard College in 1959. Kluckhohn was lecturing on Hopi ritual clowns and the imitations they perform of Navajos and other non-Hopis in the context of public ceremonials. Toward the end of his lecture, Kluckhohn remarked, "For Hopis, making fun is a way of making sense."

6. Imitation and mimicry have received relatively little

attention from anthropologists, with the result that practically nothing is known about the role of these phenomena in the communicative economies of non-Western peoples. A form of behavior that is surely universal among man, and one that is clearly recognizable among the higher primates and other mammals as well, imitation warrants systematic study if only because it seems to be a quintessential form of play. In this regard, I hope the present essay may persuade ethnographers that investigations of the uses to which imitations are put in everyday life can be well worth undertaking.

7. For a valuable discussion of indexicality in speech and its relationship to other modes of verbal signification, see Silverstein (1976).

8. The term *transformation* is used here and elsewhere exclusively in the geometrical senses of "transcription" and "transposition." Used in these senses, it should not be confused or conflated with logical and taxonomic usages currently employed by transformational linguists (e.g., Chomsky, 1965) and structural anthropologists (e.g., Lévi-Strauss, 1969).

9. These principles are described and discussed in Section 3.

10. The recognition that acts of imitation may serve important interpretive functions is by no means novel, but it has not, I think, been fully appreciated by linguistic anthropologists. A case in point is provided by Claudia Mitchell-Kernan's (1972) excellent paper on the social meanings of "marking," an Afro-American speech style in which urban Blacks in California parody the voice and mannerisms of southern rural Blacks in a fashion that is "compromising and denigrating" (p. 178). Mitchell-Kernan notes that such routines are "revealing of attitudes and values relating to lan-

guage" (p. 178), but here she chooses to let the matter rest. Consequently, the kinds of messages that "marking" performances communicate about the content of these attitudes and values – and, more specifically, about conceptions that urban Blacks have of their countrified fellows – are not discussed.

11. The idea that naturally occurring speech events may be interpreted along the lines suggested by Ricoeur and Geertz is relatively fresh, and thus its potential value for linguistic anthropology is difficult to assess. Methodological problems abound. My own view – conventional enough, but in ethnographic practice none too easy – is that one should begin by attempting to describe the principles according to which verbal texts are constructed and understood. A similar strategy appears to underlie a recent study by Mary Sanches (1975b) in which she provides an illuminating account of the sociolinguistic and proxemic rules that structure the meanings of Japanese "variety hall" performances. See also Bricker (1973, 1976) and Gossen (1976).

12. Since all meanings are in some sense cultural, the distinction drawn here between *social meanings* and *cultural meanings* has an obvious drawback: the former may be considered aspects of the latter. I use the terms as follows:

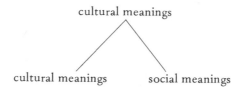

Perhaps the term *categorical meanings* could be substituted for *cultural meanings,* but here, too, misunderstandings could easily arise. My wish is simply to distinguish between two facets of metacommunicative messages: those that communicate about the conceptual content of cultural symbols, and those that communicate about the structural and affective components of situated social relationships. Although such a distinction is implicit in recent writings in sociolinguistics (Brukman, 1975; Gumperz, 1975; Sanches, 1975b; Mitchell-Kernan, 1972), it needs to be clarified, and its implications for ethnography more thoroughly explored. In general, linguistic anthropologists have tended to concentrate on the analysis of social meanings, consigning their cultural counterparts to a place of minor importance. Symbolic anthropologists have tended to do just the reverse.

13. Since the writings of Radcliffe-Brown (1940, 1949), anthropological studies of joking have focused on so-called joking relationships with the primary aim of showing that institutionalized joking in tribal societies is properly understood as a complex function of principles of kinship and marriage (Gulliver, 1957; Goody, 1959; Rigby, 1968; Kennedy, 1970; Freedman, 1972). Consequently, as Mary Douglas (1968) has pointed out, joking has only recently been studied as an activity in its own right, that is, as a distinctive mode of communication whose investigation can provide insight into the content and organization of systems of thought (cf. Beidelman, 1966). The strategy favored by most ethnographers has been to identify one or more status-role relationships in which joking is obligatory and to work "outward" from these relationships toward an understanding of broader aspects of social structure. My own approach, which is motivated by considerations similar to those of Douglas, is to start with a particular form of joking and to work "through" it toward an understanding of

the meanings of cultural symbols and the interpersonal functions served by joking itself.

14. Dan Thrapp (1967) provides a useful history of this conflict from the viewpoint of the U.S. military. Aspects of the Western Apache view are presented in Basso (1971).

15. For a more complete account of kinship and social organization in the community of Cibecue, see Basso (1970).

16. Although the characters portrayed in Western Apache joking performances are not restricted to Anglo-Americans – Blacks, Spanish-Americans, Orientals, and other Indian groups also appear – my consultants at Cibecue inform me that imitations of Whitemen have always been the most common.

17. Following Huizinga (1955), a number of writers have maintained that a defining feature of play is that it is "largely devoid of purpose" because "its outcome does not contribute to the necessary life-processes of the group" (p. 49). This may be so, but it should not be allowed to obscure the fact that, as an instrument of metacommunication and a form of social interaction, play is intrinsically purposeful and inevitably consequential (Bateson, 1972; Handelman and Kapferer, 1973; Sanches, 1975a).

18. In addition to 'jokes' (*banagozdiʔ*), the Western Apache distinguish two other major categories of 'humorous speech' (*dabagodlohé yałtiʔ*). These are (1) 'funny stories' (*dabagodlohé nagołdiʔ*), which consist of reportings of both real and fictitious events (e.g., the tale of the pubic tarantula mentioned in connection with the joking performance described in Section 1), and (2) 'teasings' or 'barbs' (*ʔenitʔįį*), which are short statements, not unlike the "one-liners" delivered by professional comedians such as Don Rickles, that

criticize the butt's character, demeanor, or personal appearance (e.g., a teenage youth to his younger sister who has just awakened and has not yet combed her hair: "Get up, you tangle-head!'").

These three categories are arranged into the taxonomy presented below.

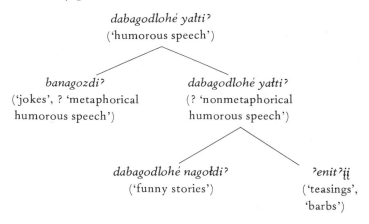

dabagodlohé yałti ʔ
('humorous speech')

banagozdi ʔ
('jokes', ? 'metaphorical humorous speech')

dabagodlohé yałti ʔ
(? 'nonmetaphorical humorous speech')

dabagodlohé nagołdi ʔ
('funny stories')

ʔenit ʔįį
('teasings', 'barbs')

Note that the expression *dabagodlohé yałti ʔ* ('humorous speech'), which operates at two levels of contrast, serves at the second level to distinguish 'jokes' from 'teasings' and 'funny stories'. The basis for this distinction, I suspect, is that whereas jokes always entail an explicit metaphorical component (i.e., the butt is depicted as something he or she is not), 'teasings' and 'funny stories' do not. If this supposition is correct, 'nonmetaphorical humorous speech' could serve as a gloss for *dabagodlohé yałti ʔ* in its most specific sense, and 'metaphorical humorous speech' could be used as an alternative gloss for *banagozdi ʔ* ('jokes').

19. The conversations presented in (1)–(3) were originally conducted in Western Apache. Exchanges (1) and (2)

were recorded in written form; (3) was recorded on tape. English translations were prepared by myself and two Apache consultants from Cibecue. Transcripts were then shown and read to participants A in (1), C and D in (2), and F and G in (3). Permission to publish the transcripts was granted by these individuals on the condition that their identities would not be revealed, and that I would emphasize that in each case they had been "only joking" and "just saying it."

20. The distinction made here between primary and secondary texts follows naturally from the observation that imitation and mimicry are forms of "keyed" or "scripted" activity. For a general discussion of keys and scriptings and their relevance to theories of the organization of social experience, see Goffman (1974: 40–82).

21. The appreciation of Western Apaches for caricature and parody is shared by other American Indian groups, including, perhaps most notably, the Pueblos. Consider, for example, the following statement by Alfonso Ortiz (1972:147): "Of burlesque and caricature generally, it can be said that they best permit insights into Pueblo modes of conception since they reveal what the Pueblos find serious or absurd, baffling or wrong, fearful or comical about life and about people. When these center about the lives of other people, they can be particularly instructive. The wonder is that this has gone almost completely unrecognized by ethnographers."

Pueblo imitations of culturally dissimilar peoples occur most conspicuously in the context of public ceremonials (Ortiz, 1972). Robert Netting (personal communication) has alerted me to the fact that a comparable tradition was present among tribes of the Northwest Coast. The Kwakiutl, for example, staged 'play potlatches' (*gwomiäsä*) that included elaborate skits in which neighboring Indian groups and Europeans were impersonated and in this manner "lampooned or derided" (Codere, 1956:340). Franz Boas, who witnessed several of these performances on Vancouver Island during the winter of 1895–96, described two of them as follows:

> After this was done, a messenger entered the house and said: "Some strangers are on the beach". The speaker of the Nā´q?oaqtôq sent a man out, who took a torch and went down to the beach. Soon he returned and informed the speaker that some white men had landed and asked to be permitted to enter. The speaker sent for them, and the messenger came back leading a young Indian girl, who was dressed up in European costume, with a gaudy hat, a velvet skirt, and a silk blouse. Then they asked NōLq?auLEla what he thought of her; if he thought she was wealthy. They asked him to send her back if she was poor. He looked at her and said: "I can easily distinguish rich and poor and I see she is wealthy. Let her stay here". Then the speaker looked at her and said: "Oh, that is Mrs. Nūle". They led her to the rear of the house and asked if she carried anything in her pocket. She produced a roll of silver quarter dollars which the speaker took and distributed among the people (Boas, 1897:559–60).

> Now the door opened, and four men dressed as policemen entered . . . The last of these acted as judge and carried a book. He sent the policemen around asking if everybody was present, and KuLE´m asked, "Are you all here?" The people replied, "Yes". Then the two other policemen

went around, looked at everybody, and stated
that one person was missing. They went out, and
soon returned leading the old woman Gudo 'yo,
whose hands were fastened with handcuffs. Then
they pretended to hold court over her on account
of her absence. The judge pretended to read the
law on the case, and fined her $70. She replied
that she was poor; that she was able to pay in
blankets but had no money. KuLE 'm, who
acted the interpreter, pretended to translate
what she said into English, and the payment of
70 blankets was accepted. Then the friends of
Gudo 'yo turned against the judge and said: "That
is always your way, policemen. As soon as you
see anyone who has money, you arrest him and
fine him". She was unchained, and the policemen
went back to the door (Boas, 1897:562–63).

Boas's materials suggest that code-switching (and
perhaps exaggerated nonverbal behavior as well) was
an integral part of all 'play potlatching' performances.
Thus, describing a skit in which a Haida Indian was
impersonated, he wrote: "A man rose who acted as
though he was a Haida. He delivered a speech, during
which he made violent gestures, imitating the sound
of the Haida language" (Boas, 1897: 546). And one
of Helen Codere's consultants recalled: "Women
pretend to be crows, then the men pretend to be
something. They 'talk Chinese' or something" (Codere,
1956: 345).

    Codere concludes her interpretation of 'play pot-
latching' among the Kwakiutl with the following
general statement. I concur with it completely.

Laughter must be regarded as the denial of cultural automation and the affirmation of a com-

plex human freedom to follow, change, or create culture. There may be no explicit analysis or evaluation in funmaking. There may be no highly conscious intellectual or emotional processes in laughter. But such elements are present, and they represent positive and creative human qualities (Codere, 1956:350).

22. In a recent statement, Geertz (1973a) has opposed his own conception of ethnography, which stresses hermeneutical forms of interpretation, to that of Ward Goodenough (1957), which emphasizes the formulation of cultural rules. Despite very real differences between these two approaches, I am not persuaded that they are incompatible. Given a class of cultural texts – and given, as Geertz (1973a:14) insists, that their meanings must be interpreted from the point of view of native actors – it follows necessarily that the ethnographer must attempt to determine how actors make sense of their texts and what kind of sense they make. In other words, he or she must try to make explicit a set of understandings, or *rules for interpretation,* that are used by the natives themselves. To the extent that Goodenough's program has drawn attention to this desideratum, and has stimulated efforts to devise a methodology for accomplishing it, it has been singularly useful and beneficial. Moreover, there is no obvious way in which it conflicts, epistemologically or otherwise, with the broader goals of cultural interpretation espoused by Geertz.

23. The attributes that distinguish the joking style of Western Apache English from its normal nonjoking counterpart are most conspicuously absent in situations where Apaches must converse with Anglo-Americans. On such occasions, feelings of incompetence and self-

consciousness tend to intrude, and English is spoken in a careful and deliberate manner, softly and slowly, with minimal variation in pitch and tone. The overall effect is one of "flatness" and lack of animation, which makes the joking style – loud, freewheeling, and exuberant – all the more striking in comparison.

24. The text of the joking encounter presented in (4) is published here with the permission of the three adults who engaged in it. Acquisition of the text on tape came by an unexpected stroke of good fortune. Earlier in the day, I had been interviewing K on matters having nothing to do with joking, and had left my recorder in her house so that we could use it again on the following day. In the evening, while K was going about her chores, she thought of something she wanted to discuss with me and decided to record it. Having done so, she was distracted by one of her children and forgot to turn off the machine, which ran on for twenty minutes more and captured J's joking imitation in its entirety. The next morning, K and I were delighted to discover her "mistake." It pleased J as well – so much so that he refused to allow me to make a transcript from the tape until he had carefully supplied the details of the nonverbal aspects of his performance.

25. Drawing heavily upon Freud's (1916) theory of humor, as well as that of Bergson (1950), Mary Douglas (1968) offers a fuller discussion of why persons out of control may seem to be funny. See also Goffman (1974:28–39).

26. Erving Goffman has pointed out to me that many of the cultural contrasts described above have to do with greeting behavior. He also notes that "a difference or misunderstanding lodged here has an especially divisive effect, for it turns Apaches off *at the point of contact.* If, in fact, you wanted to insulate your culture from an alien one, *that* would be an awfully good way to go

about it. The characterological readings, then, that Apaches give to our contact behavior are exactly the ones that best serve insulating needs" (personal communication, May 1978).

Goffman's comments are astute and persuasive, and his observation that Anglo-Americans may repel Apaches "at the point of contact" is entirely correct. The following statements from consultants at Cibecue indicate clearly just how critical the first two moments of a social encounter can be, and suggest as well that Apache interpretations of Anglo-American greeting practices may indeed serve effective insulating functions.

> Lots of Whitemen, you can tell right away they looking down at you. They look too much [i.e., stare], talk right away, shake your hand, like that. Some make lots of questions right away. No good. They just doing it for theyselves. So we try to get away fast.

> It don't take long. Pretty quick you going to know how some Whiteman is. Just how he come up to you, how he talk, ask some question, act like a big shot. He come up to you like that, act smart like that, we don't want it. So we say we got to go someplace or say we don't talk English.

> Some Whitemen learn pretty fast: how to act around Apaches. They pick it up real quick. Others have hard time. Some try to get soft with you right away, act like maybe you some Whiteman. No good. They want to be big shot, tell you what they thinking, always want to find out something about you. Right away, they do it. Some never learn to wait.

27. That peoples other than the Western Apache use joking

imitations to criticize the social behavior of Anglo-Americans – and, more interesting still, that the criticisms so registered may run along similar lines – is clearly indicated in the following statement by Mary Sanches.

> Almost all the attitudes you report as expressed by Western Apaches about 'the Whiteman' are almost identical to ones held by Japanese about *hakujin* ('whites', lit., 'white people'): (a) pushing "friendship" for ulterior motives, (b) violations of personal privacy, both verbally and nonverbally, (c) calling public attention to the obvious, etc. These comments and feelings show up in Japanese society in jokes very similar to, though not identical with, those you report, in both informal interactions (especially at parties where interaction is well-lubricated with alcohol) and in professional *rakugo* and *manzai* performances. I would bet that a lot of other groups around the world see 'the Whiteman', or 'round-eyes', or whatever the local label is, in much the same way (personal communication, April 1978).

28. This theme finds its clearest expression in the remarkable performances of Western Apache 'ritual clowns' (*łibayé*) who appear, masked and painted, in certain types of curing ceremonials. Like men who imitate Anglo-Americans in jokes, ritual clowns transform primary texts (a set of myths) into secondary texts (a representation of figures and events described in the myths). Similarly, the two major principles they employ are contrast and distortion. Clowns, however, are not permitted to speak, and therefore their performances must be accomplished entirely by means of movement, gesture, and the manipulation of physical objects by the clowns.

29. Mary Douglas (1968:365) has drawn a distinction between what she calls "standardised" jokes (e.g., "There
was a traveling salesman from Ohio . . .") and jokes
that are "spontaneous." The latter, she claims, function
to organize perceptions of social situations in ways that
the former do not. In addition, she asserts that spontaneous jokes contrast with their "standardised"
counterparts by virtue of being "morally neutral"
(p. 368). Unfortunately, what Douglas means by this
phrase is not made clear. I raise the matter because
joking imitations of Anglo-Americans, which seem to
fall nicely into Douglas's spontaneous category, are,
as Western Apaches understand them, in no sense
morally neutral. Joking imitations not only deal with
moral topics – courtesy, politeness, respect – but comment upon them in unequivocally moral terms.

30. For a clear statement on some of the instructional
functions served by symbolic dramas, see Victor
Turner (1967).

31. Lévi-Strauss (1969) has asserted that a dominant theme
in all mythology is the articulation of models of human
distinctiveness (cf. Drummond, 1977). It is clear, I
think, that Western Apache imitations of Anglo-
Americans serve a closely similar function. Perhaps this
is true of "ethnic jokes" in general.

It may also be true of song, as the following statement provided by Robert Netting (personal communication) illustrates clearly. Netting, who carried out
extensive ethnographic research among the Kofyar of
Nigeria in 1960–62, reports on a song text created by
one of his Kofyar consultants and draws attention to
the fact that code-switching, which takes place within
the text, is of fundamental importance.

The Kofyar of the Jos Plateau in northern Nigeria
have considerable contact with Hausa language

and culture. In the past, they managed to remain independent of the surrounding Hausa-Fulani states that raided the area for slaves and looked down on the indigenous people as naked pagans. With British colonial conquest after 1900, Hausa became the lingua franca of the administration and the tin mines where some Kofyar went to work. In the 1930s, a few Kofyar converted to Islam, began to wear long robes, and took up occupations such as trading, tailoring, leather working, and barbering that were learned in Hausa areas. It was said that they "became Hausa". The change in culture was reflected also in certain distinctive Moslem food taboos such as those against dog and donkey meat and those prohibiting the use of alcohol. A song sung by a young Kofyar man uses code-switching to make fun of these ethnic differences. The first phrase of each line, which states the prohibition in Hausa (italicized), is then directly contradicted by the following phrase in Kofyar. In the final line, this pattern is reversed.

Ba no cin kare, sai lua as
'I do not eat dog, except for the meat of dog'

Ba na sha giya, gai mwos maar
'I do not drink beer, except for millet beer'

Ba na cin jaki, sai lua gwa
'I do not eat donkey, except for the meat of donkey'

Gabriel Danaan *na yam mata.*
'Gabriel Danaan [Kofyar name of singer] who belongs to women' [Hausa phrase meaning 'girls like him']

32. All frames of meaning are vulnerable to what Goffman (1974:35) has termed *slippage,* a useful way of suggesting that perspectives initially taken up in relation to events may be called into question by subsequent developments that render these perspectives inapplicable. Thus, to cite a familiar example, children playing at fighting may begin to play too roughly, a development that raises the suspicion that they may not be playing at all. The possibility of slippage seems particularly prevalent where joking is concerned, for it appears to be the case that in all societies joking activity is constrained by culturally specific restrictions whose violation casts immediate doubt on the playful intentions of those who have erred and opens their actions to interpretations of a very different kind. In this connection, see Labov's (1972) fine discussion of ritual insults among Black youths in New York City.

33. Evidence for this observation comes in the form of statements by Apaches such as the following:

> X used to joke me like he was a Whiteman. I know he's just saying it, but still I don't like it.

> I never like it when somebody jokes me like a Whiteman. It makes me feel some way.

> I been joke like that lots of times. I never get used to it. The way some do it, it's too much like coming up against a Whiteman.

34. In a recent paper, Stevens (1978) observes that among the Bachama of northeastern Nigeria joking is taken as symbol of "exclusiveness of association" or, more simply, as a symbol of interpersonal unity. Stevens goes on to suggest that although joking is an "outward manifestation of an underlying relationship" (and thus what he calls a "badge of identity"), it also serves to promote the "development and preservation of the relationship

itself." These observations apply well to the Western Apache case, as, indeed, I expect they do to joking activity in most societies. However, Stevens's claim that his view of joking is new (or at least novel) seems to me to be incorrect. Similar perspectives have been clearly stated by Goffman (1974) and Labov (1972).

35. All of my Western Apache acquaintances, including those who perform joking imitations of Whitemen, acknowledge that the services provided by certain categories of Anglo-Americans (e.g., physicians) are valuable and beneficial. What is objectionable – and what joking imitations are intended to criticize – is the personally demeaning way in which these services are sometimes administered. Thus, it is not the case that Apaches fail to understand or appreciate that Anglo-Americans may be well-intentioned and genuinely anxious to help. The problem arises with how they express these intentions and go about helping.

References

Austin, John L. 1962. *How To Do Things with Words.* Oxford: Oxford University Press.

Babcock, Barbara A. 1978. Introduction to *The Reversible World: Symbolic Inversion in Art and Society,* pp. 13–36. Ed. Barbara A. Babcock. Ithaca, New York: Cornell University Press.

Basso, Keith H. 1966. "The Gift of Changing Woman." *Bulletin of the Bureau of American Ethnology,* no. 196. Washington, D.C.: Smithsonian Institution.

1969. "Western Apache Witchcraft." *Anthropological Papers of the University of Arizona,* no. 15. Tucson: University of Arizona Press.

1970. *The Cibecue Apache.* New York: Holt, Rinehart and Winston, Inc.

1971. *Western Apache Raiding and Warfare: From the Notes of Grenville Goodwin.* Tucson: University of Arizona Press.

Forthcoming. "The Western Apache." In *The Handbook of North American Indians,* vol. 9. Ed. William C. Sturtevant. Washington, D.C.: Smithsonian Institution.

Bateson, Gregory. 1972. "A Theory of Play and Fantasy." In *Steps to an Ecology of Mind,* pp. 177–93. New York: Ballantine Books.

Beidelman, Thomas O. 1966. "Utani: Some Kaguru Notions of Death, Sexuality, and Affinity." *Southwestern Journal of Anthropology* 22:33–52.

Bergson, Henri. 1950. *Le rire: Essai sur la Signification du Comique.* Paris: Presses Universitaires de France.

Blom, Jan-Petter, and John J. Gumperz. 1972. "Social Meaning in Linguistic Structures: Code-switching in Norway." In *Directions in Sociolinguistics: The Ethnography of Communication,* pp. 409–34. Ed. John J. Gumperz and Dell Hymes. New York: Holt, Rinehart and Winston, Inc.

Boas, Franz. 1897. "The Social Organization and Secret Societies of the Kwakiutl Indians." In *Report of the U.S. National Museum for 1895,* pp. 311–738. Washington, D.C.

Braroe, Niels Winther. 1975. *Indian and White: Self-Image and Interaction in a Canadian Plains Community.* Stanford, California: Stanford University Press.

Bricker, Victoria Riefler. 1973. *Ritual Humor in Highland Chiapas.* Austin: University of Texas Press.

 1976. "Some Zinacanteco Joking Strategies." In *Speech Play: Research and Resources for the Study of Linguistic Creativity,* pp. 51–62. Ed. Barbara Kirshenblatt-Gimblett. Philadelphia: University of Pennsylvania Press.

Brukman, Jan. 1975. "'Tongue Play': Constitutive and Interpretive Properties of Sexual Joking Encounters among the Koya of South India." In *Sociocultural Dimensions of Language Use,* pp. 235–67. Ed. Mary Sanches and Ben G. Blount. New York: Academic Press.

Cardinal, Harold. 1969. *The Unjust Society: The Tragedy of Canada's Indians.* Edmonton, Alberta: M.G. Hurtig, Ltd., Publishers.

Chomsky, Noam. 1965. *Aspects of the Theory of Syntax.* Cambridge, Massachusetts: M.I.T. Press.

Codere, Helen. 1956. "The Amiable Side of Kwakiutl Life." *American Anthropologist* 58:334–51.

Deloria, Vine. 1970. *Custer Died for Your Sins: An Indian Manifesto.* New York: Avon Books.

Douglas, Mary. 1968. "The Social Control of Cognition: Some Factors in Joke Perception." *Man* 3:361–76.

Drummond, Lee. 1977. "Structure and Process in the Interpretation of South American Myth: The Arawak Dog Spirit People." *American Anthropologist* 79: 842–68.

Fishman, Joshua A. 1972. "The Sociology of Language." In *Language and Social Context,* pp. 45–60. Ed. Pier Paolo Giglioli. Middlesex: Penguin Books.

Freedman, Jim. 1972. "Joking, Affinity, and the Exchange of Ritual Services among the Kiga of Northern Rwanda: An Essay on Joking Relationship Theory." *Man* 12: 154–65.

Freud, Sigmund. 1916. *Wit and Its Relation to the Unconscious.* London: Fisher and Unwin.

Garvin, Paul, ed. 1969. *A Prague School Reader.* Washington, D.C.: Georgetown University.

Geertz, Clifford. 1966. "Religion as a Cultural System." In *Anthropological Approaches to the Study of Religion,* pp. 1–46. Ed. Michael Banton. London: Tavistock Publishers, Ltd.

1973a. "Thick Description: Toward an Interpretive Theory of Culture." In *The Interpretation of Cultures: Selected Essays,* by Clifford Geertz, pp. 3–30. New York: Basic Books.

1973b. "Deep Play: Notes on the Balinese Cockfight." In *The Interpretation of Cultures: Selected Essays,* by Clifford Geertz, pp.412–53. New York: Basic Books.

1976. "'From the Native's Point of View': On the Nature of Anthropological Understanding." In *Meaning in Anthropology,* pp. 221–37. School of American Research Advanced Seminar Series. Ed. Keith H. Basso and Henry A. Selby. Albuquerque: University of New Mexico Press.

Goffman, Erving. 1974. *Frame Analysis: An Essay on the Organization of Experience.* New York: Harper & Row, Publishers.

1978. Personal communication, May 1978.

Goodenough, Ward H. 1957. "Cultural Anthropology and Linguistics." In *Report of the Seventh Annual Round Table Meeting on Linguistics and Language Study,* pp. 167–73. Ed. Paul L. Garvin. Monograph Series on Languages and Linguistics, no. 9. Washington, D.C.: Georgetown University.

Goody, Jack. 1959. "The Mother's Brother and Sister's Son in West Africa." *Journal of the Royal Anthropological Institute* 89:61–88.

Gossen, Gary H. 1976. "Verbal Dueling in Chamula." In *Speech Play: Research and Resources for the Study of Linguistic Creativity,* pp. 121–46. Ed. Barbara Kirshenblatt-Gimblett. Philadelphia: University of Pennsylvania Press.

Gulliver, P. H. 1957. "Joking Relationships in Central Africa." *Man* 57:225–38.

Gumperz, John J. 1961. "Speech Variation and the Study of Indian Civilization." *American Anthropologist* 63:976–88.

1975. Foreword to *Sociocultural Dimensions of Language Use,* pp. xi–xxi. Ed. Mary Sanches and Ben G. Blount. New York: Academic Press.

1976. "The Sociolinguistic Significance of Conversational Code-Switching." In *Papers on Language and Context,* by Jenny Cook-Gumperz and John J. Gumperz, pp. 1–46. Working Paper No. 46, Language Behavior Research Laboratory. Mimeographed. Berkeley: University of California, Berkeley.

Gumperz, John J. and Eduardo Hernandez-Chavez. 1971.

"Cognitive Aspects of Bilingualism." In *Language Use and Language Change,* pp. 111–25. Ed. W. H. Whiteley. London: Oxford University Press.

1972. "Bilingualism, Bidialectalism, and Classroom Interaction." In *Functions of Language in the Classroom,* pp. 84–108. Ed. Courtney B. Cazden, Vera P. John, and Dell Hymes. New York: Teachers College Press.

Handelman, Don and Bruce Kapferer. 1973. "Forms of Joking Activity: A Comparative Approach." *American Anthropologist* 74:484–517.

Highwater, Jamake. 1976. *Song from the Earth: American Indian Painting.* Boston: New York Graphic Society.

Huizinga, Johan. 1955. *Homo Ludens: A Study of the Play Element in Culture.* Boston: Beacon Press. (First published in 1950.)

Hymes, Dell. 1974a. "Social Anthropology, Sociolinguistics, and the Ethnography of Speaking." In *Foundations in Sociolinguistics: An Ethnographic Approach,* pp. 83–117. Philadelphia: University of Pennsylvania Press.

1974b. "Studying the Interaction of Language and Social Life." In *Foundations in Sociolinguistics: An Ethnographic Approach,* pp. 29–66. Philadelphia: University of Pennsylvania Press.

Kaut, Charles R. 1957. "The Western Apache Clan System: Its Origins and Development." *University of New Mexico Publications in Anthropology,* no. 9. Albuquerque: University of New Mexico Press.

Kazin, Alfred. 1972. "The Human Comedy." In *The Critic as Artist: Essays on Books (1920-1970),* pp. 220–28. Ed. Gilbert A. Harrison. New York: Liveright.

Kennedy, John G. 1970. "Bonds of Laughter among the Tarahumara Indians: Toward the Rethinking of Joking Relationship Theory." In *The Social Anthropology of Latin America: Essays in honor of Ralph Leon Beals,* pp. 36–68. Ed. Walter Goldschmidt and Harry Hoijer. Berkeley: University of California Press.

Labov, William. 1972. "Rules for Ritual Insults." In *Studies in Social Interaction,* pp. 120–69. Ed. David Sudnow. New York: The Free Press.

Lambert, Wallace E. 1971. "A Social Psychology of Bilingualism." In *Language Use and Language Change,* pp. 95–110. Ed. W. H. Whiteley, London: Oxford University Press.

Lévi-Strauss, Claude. 1969. *The Raw and the Cooked (Mythologiques I).* Trans. John and Doreen Weightman. New York: Harper & Row, Publishers.

Mitchell-Kernan, Claudia. 1972. "Signifying and Marking: Two Afro-American Speech Acts." In *Directions in Sociolinguistics: The Ethnography of Communication,* pp. 163–79. Ed. John J. Gumperz and Dell Hymes. New York: Holt, Rinehart and Winston, Inc.

Momaday, N. Scott. 1969. *House Made of Dawn.* New York: Harper and Row, Publishers.

Netting, Robert M. 1978. Personal communication, October 1978.

Ortiz, Alfonso. 1972. "Ritual Drama and Pueblo World View." In *New Perspectives on the Pueblos,* pp. 135–62. Ed. Alfonso Ortiz. School of American Research Advanced Seminar Series. Albuquerque: University of New Mexico Press.

Ortiz, Simon. 1974. "Relocation." In *Voices from Wah'kontah: Contemporary Poetry of Native Americans,* pp. 82–3. Ed. Robert K. Dodge and Joseph B. McCullough. New York: International Publishers.

Parmee, Edward A. 1968. *Formal Education and Culture Change: A Modern Apache Indian Community and Government Education Programs.* Tucson: University of Arizona Press.

Radcliffe-Brown, A. R. 1940. "On Joking Relationships." *Africa* 13:195–210.

1949. "A Further Note on Joking Relationships." *Africa* 19:133–40.

Ricoeur, Paul. 1973. "The Model of the Text: Meaningful Action Considered as a Text." *New Literary History* 5:91–120.

Rigby, P. 1968. "Joking Relationships, Kin Categories, and Clanship among the Gogo." *Africa* 38:133–54.

Rubin, Joan. 1962. "Bilingualism in Paraguay." *Anthropological Linguistics* 4:52–8.

1968. *National Bilingualism in Paraguay.* The Hague: Mouton.

Sanches, Mary. 1975a. "Metacommunicative Acts and Events: Introduction." In *Sociocultural Dimensions of Language Use,* pp. 163–76. Ed. Mary Sanches and Ben G. Blount. New York: Academic Press.

1975b. "Falling Words: An Analysis of a Japanese *Rakugo* Performance." In *Sociocultural Dimensions of Language Use,* pp. 269–306. Ed. Mary Sanches and Ben G. Blount. New York: Academic Press.

1978. Personal communication, April 1978.

Schneider, David M. 1968. *American Kinship: A Cultural Account.* Englewood Cliffs, N.J.: Prentice-Hall.

1976. "Toward a Theory of Culture." In *Meaning in Anthropology,* pp. 197–220. Ed. Keith H. Basso and Henry A. Selby. School of American Research Advanced Seminar Series. Albuquerque: University of New Mexico Press.

Schutz, Alfred. 1944. "The Stranger: An Essay in Social Psychology." *American Journal of Sociology* 49:499–507.

1953. "Common Sense and Scientific Interpretation in Human Action." *Philosophy and Phenomenological Research* 14:1–37.

1954. "Concept and Theory Formation in the Social Sciences." *The Journal of Philosophy* 51:257–74.

1964. "Equality and Meaning Structure of the Social

World." In *The Collected Papers of Alfred Schutz.* Volume 2, pp. 226–73. Ed. Maurice Natanson. The Hague: Nijhoff.

Silko, Leslie Marmon. 1977. *Ceremony.* New York: Viking Press.

Silverstein, Michael. 1976. "Shifters, Linguistic Categories, and Cultural Description." In *Meaning in Anthropology,* pp. 11–55. Ed. Keith H. Basso and Henry A. Selby. School of American Research Advanced Seminar Series. Albuquerque: University of New Mexico Press.

Spicer, Edward H. 1967. *Cycles of Conquest.* Tucson: University of Arizona Press. (Second Printing.)

Stevens, Jr., Philip. 1978. "Bachama Joking Categories: Toward New Perspectives in the Study of Joking Relationships." *Journal of Anthropological Research* 34:47–71.

Thrapp, Dan L. 1967. *The Conquest of Apacheria.* Norman: University of Oklahoma Press.

Turner, Victor. 1967. "Betwixt and Between: The Liminal Period in *Rites de Passage.*" In *The Forest of Symbols: Aspects of Ndembu Ritual,* pp. 93–111. Ithaca, New York: Cornell University Press.

Walsh, Marnie. 1974. "Emmet Kills-Warrior: Turtle Mountain Reservation." In *Voices from Wah'kon-tah: Contemporary Poetry of Native Americans,* pp. 106–8. Ed. Robert K. Dodge and Joseph B. McCullough. New York: International Publishers.

Welch, James. 1974. *Winter in the Blood.* New York: Harper & Row, Publishers.